CREDITOCRACY

AND THE CASE FOR

DEBT REFUSAL

CREDIT OCRACY

AND THE CASE FOR DEBT REFUSAL

ANDREW ROSS

O/R

OR Books
New York · London

Published by OR Books, New York and London
Visit our website at www.orbooks.com

First printing 2013

Cataloging-in-Publication data is available from the Library of Congress.
A catalog record for this book is available from the British Library.

ISBN 978-1-939293-38-1 paperback
ISBN 978-1-939293-39-8 e-book

This book is set in the typeface Bembo.
Text design by Bathcat Ltd. Typeset by Lapiz Digital, Chennai, India.
Printed by BookMobile in the United States and CPI Books Ltd in the United Kingdom.

CONTENTS

YOU ARE NOT A LOAN

#STRIKEDEBT

ACKNOWLEDGMENTS

Many fellow activists in the debt resistance movement contributed ideas, arguments, inspiration, and community love to this book. They include George Caffentzis, Chris Casuccio, Ann Larson, Pam Brown, Astra Taylor, Laura Hanna, Yates McKee, David Graeber, Aaron Bornstein, Thomas Gokey, Suzanne Collado, Sue Meaney, Amin Husain, Nitasha Dhillon, Nick Mirzeoff, Marisa Holmes, Chris Brown, Aleksandra Perisic, Sarah McDaniel, Matt Presto, Andrew Hiller, Christina Daniel, Shyam Khanna, Jacques Laroche, Hilary Goodfriend, Brian Kalbrenner, Nicole Hala, Luke Herrine, Christine Nyland, Sean McAlpin, Cristian Mejia, Sandy Nurse, Jerry Goralnick, Jim Constanzo, Mike Andrews, Steven Tran-Creque, Max Cohen, Ryan Hickey, Robert Oxford, Doug Barrett, Nick Katevich, Mike Monicelli, Sara Burke, Justin Wedes, Monica Johnson, Hannah Appel, Biola Jeje, Matthew Tinker, Rene Gabri, Ayreen Anastas, Bill Talen, Jacques Servin, Sylvia Federici, Ashley Dawson, Marina Sitrin, Nathan Schneider, Austin Guest, Mark Read, Malav Kanuga,

Morgan Buck, Conor Tomas Reed, Zak Greene, Ingrid Burrington, Leina Bocar, Chris Kasper, Annie Spencer, Nina Mehta, Kylie Benton-Connell, Zoltan Gluck, Michele Hardesty, Isham Christie, Christy Thornton, Stuart Schrader, Daniel Cohen, and fellow jailbirds, Laurel Ptak and Matthew Connors.

Writers who have been fellow travelers on the killing fields of debt include Sarah Jaffe, Mike Konczal, Cryn Johannsen, Alan Collinge, Steve Fraser, Richard Dienst, Michael Hardt, Chris Newfield, Tamara Draut, Samir Sonti, Adolph Reed, Jeff Williams, Fred Moten, Anya Kamenetz, Nick Pinto, Seth Ackerman, Pam Martens, and Rachel Signer.

Many thanks to NYU comrades from the FASP core, who include Marie Monaco, Mark Miller, Rebecca Karl, Molly Nolan, Bertell Ollman, Christine Harrington, Adam Becker, Jeff Goodwin, Jim Uleman, Angela Zito, Patrick Deer, Bo Riccobono, Denis Geronimus, Anna McCarthy, Robby Cohen, Steve Duncombe, Barbara Weinstein, Michael Reckenwald, Ernest Davis, Danielle Holke, and Linda Gross,

It was a great pleasure to work again with my editor and friend Colin Robinson (YNWA), and with John Oakes. Natasha Lewis, Emily Freyer, Justin Humphries and Courtney Andujar were a superb team at OR Books. I'm also grateful to Jackson Smith for his assistance with preparing the manuscript.

On the home front, Maggie was a nonstop affirmer, even when she feigned being an "Occupy widow." And all hail to Zola and Stella for stepping up to be the original Little Red Squares.

INTRODUCTION

From April to June 2013, U.S. banks recorded their highest-ever profits for a quarter—$42.2 billion. Even those who routinely cheer every report of higher earnings had reason to pause. Maybe this was one piece of upside financial news that should not be ballyhooed. For one thing, the lion's share of the profits went to just six banks (Bank of America, Citigroup, Wells Fargo, JPMorgan Chase, Goldman Sachs, and Morgan Stanley), all of them larger and more powerful than they were before their institutional greed helped to decimate the global economy in 2008. Five years after the financial collapse, their capacity to operate beyond the reach of regulators was even more apparent. On March 6, 2013, U.S. Attorney General Eric Holder confessed to the Senate Judiciary Committee that when banks acquire so much concentrated power, it is "difficult for us to prosecute them … if you do bring a criminal charge, it will have a negative impact on the national economy, perhaps even the global economy." Was it refreshing or just plain alarming to hear the nation's top law enforcement official frankly acknowledge how helpless he was in the face of the "too big to fail" (now seen as too-big-to-jail) doctrine that had served the bankers so well even as it caused a worldwide depression?

Using international accounting rules, the combined assets of the big six totaled $14.7 trillion (or 93 percent of U.S. GDP in 2012), while the entirety of the country's banking assets was worth 170 percent of GDP. In Europe, the situation was even more acute; Germany's banking sector, for example, clocked in at 326 percent of national GDP, while the go-go U.K. banks were at 492 percent.[1] The exposure of American banks to derivatives alone had increased to $232 trillion, almost a third more than before 2008 when the escalation of these risky bets helped to bring on the financial crash. Those figures are much more telling than the ratio of overall national debt to GDP, though the latter has commanded all the attention, and has been cynically and unjustifiably seized on by deficit hawks as an excuse to crank up the engines of austerity. Just as chilling was the news that the big six U.S. banks collectively were carrying a debt load of $8.7 trillion. With that combination of debt overhead, exposure to dodgy derivatives, leverage over the national economy, and continued weak regulatory oversight, there is a very high risk of a repeat of the 2008 meltdown. Indeed, many industry insiders believe that an equally ruinous relapse is already in the making.

Holder's admission that the government lacked the wherewithal to punish bankers for their widely publicized record of extortion was a significant milestone, particularly for a democracy that has long struggled to contain the damage inflicted by plutocrats in its midst. The ability of Wall Street barons to hold the government in thrall is nothing new.[2] In a 1933 letter, Franklin D. Roosevelt wrote: "The real truth of the matter is, as you and I know, that a financial element in the large centers has owned the government ever since the days of Andrew Jackson."[3] Owning lawmakers may be a venerable prerogative for American financiers, but the rise of a full-blown creditocracy is more recent. Financialization had to creep into every corner of the household economy before the authority of the creditor class took on a sovereign, unassailable character.

In other words, it is not enough for every social good to be turned into a transactional commodity, as is the case in a rampant market civilization. A creditocracy emerges when the cost of each of these goods, no matter how staple, has to be debt-financed, and when indebtedness becomes the precondition not just for material improvements in the quality of life, but for the basic requirements of life. Financiers seek to wrap debt around every possible asset and income stream, ensuring a flow of interest from each. Furthermore, when fresh sources of credit are routinely needed to service existing debt (neatly captured in the 1990s bumper sticker, "I Use MasterCard to Pay Visa"),[4] we can be sure we are entering a more advanced phase of creditor rule. For the working poor, this kind of compulsory indebtedness is a very familiar arrangement, and has long outlived its classic expression under feudalism, indenture, and slavery. Each of these systems of debt bondage were followed by kindred successors—sharecropping, company scrip, loan sharking—and their legacy is alive and well today on the subprime landscape of fringe finance, where "poverty banks" operate in every other storefront on Loan Alley. But the bonds created by household debt have also spread upwards and now affect the majority of the population, tethering two generations of the college educated. With total U.S. consumer debt at a whopping $11.13 trillion (U.S. GDP in 2012 was $15.68 trillion), 77 percent of households are in serious debt, and one in seven Americans is being, or has been, pursued by a debt collector.[5] As for the beneficiaries, the tipping point for a creditocracy occurs when "economic rents"—from debt-leveraging, capital gains, manipulation of paper claims through derivatives, and other forms of financial engineering—are no longer merely a supplementary source of income, but have become the most reliable and effective instrument for the amassing of wealth and influence.

GRAND THEFT BANKING

All of the available evidence, and much of our own experience—whether we serve in high elected office or languish as empty-handed targets of a collection agency—suggests that a full-blown creditocracy is now in place, and it is distinct from earlier forms of monopoly capitalism in which profits from production dominated.[6] There are many ways of illustrating this historic development. Consider the balance of power between banks and government. In 1895, J.P. Morgan was called upon to save the U.S. Treasury from default (and again in 1907), but the shoe was on the other foot by 2008, when the Treasury was forced to bail out JPMorgan Chase, and few doubt that it would be obliged to do so again in the future. The shift is also displayed in how corporations make profits. Jumbo firms, like GE and GM, which commanded the economy on the strength of their industrial production, have become much more dependent for their revenue on their firms' respective finance arms. Companies are no longer regarded primarily as worthy recipients of productive loans for tangible outputs but as targets for leveraged buyouts, to be loaded down with debt and ruthlessly used to extract finance fees and interest. The difference between Mitt Romney's career, at Bain Capital, and his father's, at the American Motor Company, neatly summarizes this transition from industrial to financial capitalism.[7] As for ordinary individuals, we are now under constant financial surveillance by the major credit bureaus (Equifax, Experian, and TransUnion), whose credit reports, scores, and ratings of our conduct as debtors control the gateways to so many areas of economic need and want. Operating outside of public oversight, these agencies answer only to the requirements of the creditor class, and the profiles they assign to us are like ID tags, marking our rank and class, in the present and in the years to come, since they are used to predict future behavior.

We know that more and more of the 99 percent are suffering from undue debt burdens—in the form of financial claims that can never be repaid—but is it so clear who belongs to the class of creditors? Following Margaret Thatcher's promotion of "pension fund capitalism," the pension funds of workers have also been drawn into the financial markets. Indeed, these funds now hold a significant portion of the public debt, especially municipal debt, currently being used as a justification for pushing through austerity policies. In a formal and legal sense, the workers are creditors, and they stand to lose if the debts are written off indiscriminately in a bankruptcy proceeding. In accord with the "popular capitalist" mentality encouraged by Thatcher and her neoliberal successors, their investments, like all others, are exposed to risk. Indeed, pension funds managers are forced to make highly speculative investments to meet their long-term promises (as much as 8 percent in annual returns) to contributors, and so they entrust the assets to Wall Street hucksters looking to charge inflated fees and offload high-risk derivatives. Company pension funds are routinely looted by corporate raiders, and state pension funds have become an especially ripe target for employers or governments in search of cash to balance their books, or assets to turn over to hedge funds and private equity funds.

But the business of investing savings for retirement has little bearing on workers' primary identity as waged labor, though contradictions clearly arise when the investments are handled by Wall Street funds that inflict damage on workers' interests in general. Even if the annuities do turn out as promised, decades hence, the recipients have not been generating their main income from investment, as is the case for the principal beneficiaries of a creditocracy. Workers who are part of the "real" economy, and whose household debts have risen while their wages stagnated, do not really inhabit the same world as the players who live off unearned income in the undertaxed world of financial engineering. Data analysis of the net transfer of wealth to the *bona fide* 1 percent creditors has shown how decisive the economic rents are to the income of the latter and to their ownership of capitalism. Extraction of these rents are the reason why this sliver of the population has captured most of the income growth over the last three decades and virtually all of it over the last five years.[8] For sure, the diversification of pension funds and the growth of 401(k) retirement plans mean that many more of us who do productive work in the real economy are tied into the world of finance than was once the case. But this circumstance has not substantially altered our sense of being in the world, and it is far outweighed by our ensnarement, like everyone else we know, in the bankers' debt trap.

Banks, brokerages, hedge funds, private equity firms, and all the other entities that operate in the shadow banking system have an interest in gathering influence and immunity for themselves, but they are first and foremost tools of accumulation for their owners, clients, shareholders, and direct beneficiaries. As such, their business is to grab as much of the economic surplus as they can by keeping everyone else in debt, for as long as possible. The build-up in all kinds of debt—sovereign, commercial, and household—that led to the financial collapse has slowed in some sectors—housing most notably—but the escalation continues in the fields of healthcare, auto loans, and especially in education, where the U.S. national aggregate will soon approach $1.2 trillion. It is customary to lament that these obligations will never be paid off. This prospect may be distressing to some, but that is beside the point. Citizens of a creditocracy are not expected, nor are they encouraged, to pay off *all* their debts. After all, we are no longer useful to creditors if we somehow manage to wipe the slate clean. The point is to prolong our debt service until the bitter end, and even beyond the grave, as is the case for loan co-signers. The sober truth is that debts, especially at compound interest, multiply at a much faster rate than the ability to repay. Original lenders are all too aware of this, which is why they sell on the loans as fast they can.

Managing the lifelong burden of debt service is now an existential condition for the majority, but what about its impact on citizenship? How can a democracy survive when it is on the road to debt serfdom? The history of the struggle for political liberty is closely tied to the growth of credit. As James MacDonald has argued, the democratic institutions of liberal societies were able to survive and flourish because government bonds made it possible to borrow cheaply, especially in times of war.[9] But today's bond markets, which are globally networked and susceptible to speculative bets from hedge funds, are more likely to "judge," "discipline," and "reward" policymakers than to faithfully serve their ends. Central banks increasingly act to ensure the solvency of banks, and not sovereign governments trying to cope with public deficits. The high and mighty presumption of creditors to be made whole now routinely overrides the responsibility of elected national representatives to carry out the popular will, resulting in "failed democracies" all over the world. Even Mario Monti, the placid technocrat appointed in 2012 as Italian prime minister to dampen popular opposition to financial power, spoke out against what he called the emergence of a "creditocracy" in Europe. He was referring specifically to how sovereign governance was being circumvented by the priority given to foreign bondholders, as represented through the big German, French, Swiss, and Dutch banks.

The fledgling civic republicanism of a country like the U.S. ought to have fostered a moral economy of debt, ensuring fair terms and treatment between lenders and borrowers, and equal measures of protection when insolvency occurred. But creditors have always been given the upper hand.[10] In his day, Jefferson was hardly alone in denouncing the predatory conduct of speculators, and wishing for an end to the debt peonage that still plagued the Old World. In particular, he considered it a natural right to be freed of the debts of a previous generation, as "a salutary curb on the spirit of war and indebtment. The modern theory of the perpetuation of debt has drenched the earth with blood and crushed its inhabitants under burdens ever accumulating."[11] Yet the new republic's first order of business was to figure out who would foot the bill for the Revolutionary War debts. Efforts to pass on the costs in taxes to yeoman farmers provoked armed uprisings, first in Shays' Rebellion in central and western Massachusetts (the insurgents closed courts and liberated debtors from prisons) and later during the Whiskey Rebellion in eastern Pennsylvania.

The specter of Shays' insurrectionary farmer-debtors was one of the reasons why the framers hastened to adopt a constitution that limited democracy and enshrined property protection as the overriding function of government. As for the slavery compromise reached by the delegates in Independence Hall, that baneful outcome was not far removed from the circuits of debt bondage that launched the slave trade in Africa, and from which white property owners and their descendants in several nations would continue to benefit. In the course of the nineteenth century, the American ideal of republican independence was further undercut by the experience of farmers' mass indebtedness to Wall Street banks, insolvency in the face of exorbitant and unpayable demands, and imprisonment at the dictate of creditors. The lopsided creditor-debtor relationship, reinforced by bankruptcy laws that still overwhelmingly favor lenders, is one of the more grisly illustrations of the gulf between the creed of political freedom and the reality of American life.

The concern that political ideals are imperiled by debt servitude is, of course, much older than the founding of the American republic. The historical record shows that a society unable to check the power of the creditor class will quickly see the onset of debt bondage; democracies segue into oligarchies, credit becomes a blunt instrument for absorbing more and more economic surplus, and rents are extracted from non-productive assets. Are we heading down this path, once again? Many commentators are saying as much when they point to the revival of debtors' prisons, or condemn student debt as a form of indenture, or compare banking practices, on Wall Street as well as on Loan Alley, to the most extreme forms of usury. So, too, the revival of interest in a debt

Strike Debt digital meme, July 2012

jubilee (or mass debt forgiveness) not only in developing countries, but also in the global North, is evocative of macro-solutions hatched in the ancient world by rulers who were so desperate to restore the balance of popular power in their favor that they abolished all existing debts, freed debt slaves, and returned land to original owners.

This kind of talk is indicative of the extremity of the current debt crisis. All the evidence shows that drastic relief measures are needed, and that a new kind of non-extractive economy, benefiting from what Keynes called the "euthanasia of the *rentier*," ought to be built. Pursuing that alternative path—to a society guided by the productive use of credit—may be the only way of salvaging democracy. But for establishment economists, even those who question the credo of neoliberalism, there is no crisis, only a debt "overhang" that needs to be reduced to manageable levels before the normal pattern of debt-financed growth can reassert itself.

In the final chapter of this book, I show why there is no viable return to that debt-growth formula. After incomes stagnated in the 1970s, respectable growth rates could only be achieved through a series of speculative asset bubbles. Each time the bubble burst, we could see how the formula rested on an insubstantial foundation. As far as lasting prosperity goes, it is fair to conclude that much of the growth was fake, producing only phony wealth, and that future efforts to inflate prices will end the same way. But from an ecological perspective, there is little doubt that this pattern is entirely unsustainable. There now exists a mountain of scientific evidence, beginning with the seminal 1974 report, *Limits to Growth,* which testifies to the calamitous impact of GDP-driven growth on the biosphere. Restoring business as usual, once that pesky "overhang" disappears, can only be a recipe for eco-collapse.

As with any unjust social arrangement, a creditocracy has to be stripped of its legitimacy in the public mind before its actual hold on power is dissolved. How far along this road have we come? Given the battering that bankers have taken over the past five years, it's a testament to their self-projected mystique that they still command even a fraction of their standing as indispensable members of society. Every other day brings a fresh headline about their misconduct and profiteering, as swindle after swindle is uncovered. The judicial investigations multiply, producing few convictions (and only of junior employees), but an ever-longer roster of fines, refunds, and other penalties. Some of the settlements to end the criminal and civil charges are massive. By the fall of 2013, JPMorgan Chase, for example, was in negotiations with the U.S. Justice Department over a $13 billion settlement for packing mortgage-backed securities with dodgy home loans. Notably, less than $2 billion looked like it would be claimed in fines and only $4 billion in relief for homeowners, while more than $7 billion was being allocated for investors who suffered losses.[12] In any event, the profits of JPMorgan and its peers are so large that such penalties are shrugged off as the cost of doing business. Public trust, the crucial quality that banks have customarily relied on in order to trade, has long been decimated; we have come to regard their ingenious financial products as little more than scams, and we know that the bill for all of their risky conduct will likely end up with us. Yet the banks retain their cachet as institutions that are just too indispensable to reform, let alone transform into socially beneficial entities, and most importantly, their lobbying firepower ensures that legislators will always look out for their interests.

In *The Bankers' New Clothes*, Anat Admati and Martin Hellwig argue that "there is a pervasive myth that banks and banking are special and different from all other companies in the economy. Anyone who questions the mystique and the claims that are made is at risk of being declared incompetent to participate in the discussion."[13] Finance, we are encouraged to believe, is too complex for lay people to understand. One of the outcomes of this mystique is that too many of us are trapped in the payback mindset. Though we may be more and more aware of the irresponsibility and fraud of big creditors who won't pay their own debts, and who offload all their risky loans to others, we still accept that it is immoral to fail to repay our debts to them. Of course, there are lawyers, courts, and police standing at the ready to enforce this payback morality, and a ruined credit score to live with in the case of a default. But these are instruments of coercion; they serve as backups if the mechanism of consent falters. When the psychology of the consenting debtor shifts, as it is now slowly doing, from resignation to reluctance, and even to resistance, then the authority of the creditors' self-interested moralism begins to lose its sway. Then, and only then, are we able to honestly question whether we owe anything at all to people and institutions that, were it not for the figment of the banker's new clothes, would rightly be seen as engaged in extortion.

ABOLISHING THE DEBT SENTENCE

More public education is needed about how creditor rule is upheld, and it is in that spirit that this book makes the case for the refusal of household debts. When a government cannot protect its people from the harms inflicted by rent extractors, and when debt burdens become an existential threat to a free citizenry, then the refusal to pay back is a defensible act of civil disobedience. For those aiming to reinvent democracy, this refusal may be nothing short of a responsibility. The case for debt cancellation in developing countries has already been made by groups within or allied to the Jubilee South movement.[14] These advocates have devised moral and legal arguments for repudiating the external debts of governments, and have had some success in delivering relief for some of the world's poorest populations. Public debts in the global North are now at the core of the austerity policies being implemented from the battered periphery of the Eurozone to the beleaguered cohort of ex-industrial cities like Detroit and Baltimore. The process of questioning which of these debts is legitimate—and deserving of repayment—and which are unfair impositions—to be rightfully rejected—is already underway.[15] Now is the time, as I argue in this book, to extend this process to household debts, especially those taken on simply to gain access to basic social goods.

In what follows, I summarize some of the arguments underpinning the case for debt refusal. Most appeal to broad moral principles, as opposed to quantifiable rules, but there is no reason why these principles could not be applied in a way that would produce some hard numbers:

- Loans which either benefit the creditor only, or inflict social and environmental damage on individuals, families, and communities, should be renegotiated to compensate for harms.
- The sale of loans to borrowers who cannot repay is unscrupulous, and so the collection of such debts should not be honored.
- The banks, and their beneficiaries, awash in profit, have done very well; they have been paid enough already, and do not need to be additionally reimbursed.
- The credit was not theirs to begin with—most of it was obtained through the dubious power of money creation, thanks to fractional reserve banking and the "magic" of derivatives. The right to claim unearned income from debts created so easily should not be recognized as binding.
- Even if household debts were not intentionally imposed as political constraints, they unavoidably stifle our capacity to think freely, act conscientiously, and fulfill our democratic responsibilities. Economic disobedience is justified as a protective deed on behalf of democracy.

- Extracting long-term profits from our short-term need to access subsistence resources or vital common goods like education, healthcare, and public infrastructure is usurious, and should be outlawed.
- Each act of debt service should be regarded as a non-productive addition to the banks' balance sheets and a subtraction from the "real" economy that creates jobs, adequately funds social spending, and sustains the well-being of communities.
- Obliging debtors to forfeit future income is a form of wage theft, and, if the debts were incurred simply to prepare ourselves, in mind and body, for employment, they should be resisted.
- Given the fraud and deceit practiced by bankers, and the likelihood that they will not refrain from such anti-social conduct in the future, it would be morally hazardous of us to reward them any further.

The foregoing is not an exhaustive list, but it is a start, and I offer it with an invitation to add others. Through the reasoned combination of these moral arguments with more practical principles of measurement, it will be possible to determine which debts should be refused, and which should be honored. Most important of all, debtors who stand together, with the spirited support of a broad movement behind them, can make the strongest moral case. Negotiating with creditors on an individual basis might win some personal relief but will not alter, let alone supplant, the norms of conduct that sustain a creditocracy.

Once the public psychology around debt has decisively shifted away from automatic compliance with payback morality, how will the new mindset translate into action? When there is no prospect of debt relief issuing from the government, debtors will have to take it for themselves, and by any means necessary. Millions default on their household debts annually, and are privately punished for the outcome. A collective default, in the form of a mass debt strike, seems unlikely from our current vantage point, though there is little doubt it would have a sharp political impact. Organizing around debt is not easy—each debtor's situation is like a fingerprint—but the conditions for the emergence of a debtors' movement have seldom been more auspicious.[16] Even though we cannot predict, at this point, what form it will take, which pathways it will pursue, and which tactics it will adopt, the need for such a movement is self-evident. For those who like neat distinctions, the historical moment can be summarized as follows. Whereas strife over wages was central to the industrial era, the grand conflict of our times is shaping up as the struggle over debt, and any just resolution calls for a level of organizing at least as momentous as the labor movement in its heyday.

The rejection of existing illegitimate debts is not enough, of course. Wiping the slate clean, in and of itself, will not alter the continuing use of debt-leveraging to redistribute wealth upwards and constrain democracy downwards. Debt cancellation is only the first step. An alternative economy, run on socially productive credit, has to materialize if the control over economic planning by Wall Street and other banking centers is to be decisively loosened. To most people, that is a daunting prospect, because it evokes some colossal overhaul of the current system that could only be achieved through the capture of state power. Yet many of the institutions and practices that support an alternative economy already exist and are thriving in their own right. Mutualist, non-profit, commons-based, and community-oriented, their economic impact is already much larger, in the aggregate, than is generally acknowledged. Credit unions, workers' cooperatives, and community-supported agriculture are well established and expanding in membership everywhere, while more experimental practices involving time banks, social money, and community currencies are being tried out in places, like Greece and Spain, where the mainstream economy has collapsed. Building on these existing commonist initiatives may be easier than halting the neoliberal privatization of the public sector, but, for some social goods—education, healthcare, infrastructure, and energy among them—public provision is still critical. An alternative economy should be a mixed one, public and commonist. Whatever the ratio of the mix, there should be no place, and no need, for most of the frenzied rent-seeking activity that feeds the financial services industry.

A successor economy cannot sustain itself without new forms of political expression and association. Historically, creditors needed a representative government to ensure that the citizenry would agree to the repayment of public debts:

as borrowers, absolute monarchs had been fickle about their obligations. "Since the Renaissance," Michael Hudson observes, "bankers have shifted their political support to democracies. This did not reflect egalitarian or liberal political convictions as such, but rather a desire for better security for their loans."[17] Democratic governments proved to be more reliable clients, though they still defaulted on sovereign debts on a regular basis—more than 250 times since 1800, according to one estimate.[18] But today's legislators are more and more exposed as helpless in the face of creditors' demands, and incapable of checking the power of high finance over policy-making. Too many younger people now see the current exercise of representative democracy as a rotten end-game. It has stopped being meaningful, and not just because of the hijacking of power on the part of the creditor class. Younger activists have been practicing democracy in different ways—often labeled horizontalist—since the late 1990s. Leaderless process in decision-making and action is now a default mentality for at least one generation, as are the social customs of cooperative networking and mutual aid.[19] Perhaps we should no longer refer to these as experimental practices, "prefigurative" of a more humane future. Among the politically aware, they have become quite normative, and are likely to work their way into the main currents of civil society in the years to come. When this happens, we will see if the impersonal relations of money debt can actually be transformed into warm social bonds—mutually nourishing debts, in other words, that we owe each other in the exercise of our freedoms.

I am not an economist, and the financial knowledge I draw on in these pages is not the preserve of a specialist. Much of my understanding of credit comes from my self-education as a participant in the debt resistance initiatives that emerged from Occupy Wall Street and the other worldwide movements from 2011 onward. Moreover, this book is a work of moral commentary and political advocacy, not academic analysis, though it does rest on scholarly research. For example, I discuss the merits of debt auditing, but do not offer advanced technical protocols for determining which debts are illegitimate, and which should be honored. That work still needs to be done, building on the moral principles of repudiation laid out here. With few exceptions, the book does not feature the voices or stories of debtors themselves; they are readily available on the Internet, and elsewhere. But it was directly inspired by the open expression of their cause—an eloquent outpouring of pent-up woe, resentment, and solidarity, widely seen as a coming-out moment for those no longer silenced by the shame and guilt that is the debtor's lot. Last, but not least, the arguments advanced in these pages came out of the shared discussion and direct actions of comrades in Strike Debt and the Occupy Student Debt Campaign, who responded to the moment.[20] In that regard, it is a movement book, even though the movement is still finding its voice, and feet.

WE ARE ALL REVOLVERS

In 1975, an infamous report for the Trilateral Commission suggested that Western elites were confronting a new menace that the authors described as an "excess of democracy." According to the report, electorates were no longer content to be passively governed, and so all kinds of demands were being made by newly emboldened populations—women, gays, ethnic minorities, the urban poor, students, and the aspiring citizenry of decolonized countries. This "overloading" of government by ordinarily apathetic citizens was unhealthy, in the opinion of the report's authors. The industrialized countries, they concluded, needed "a greater degree of moderation in democracy." Otherwise, all of these new demands would foment a revolution of rising expectations.[1]

The message about clamping down on these insurgent voices was ominous enough, though it was submerged in all the attention garnered by the Trilateral Commission's status as a favorite target of conspiracy theorists in the decades to come.[2] The commission's roster of unelected movers and shakers—business tycoons, politician heavyweights, and strenuous policy intellectuals—got so much lip service from right-wing vigilantes in a froth about one-world government that its tangible impact on elite opinion and policymaking went largely unacknowledged. As it happens, this discreet cabal was just one of the many unelected, international bodies—the World Trade Organization, European Commission, World Intellectual Property Organization, the G8, the Troika—that have emerged in the interim to operate beyond the accountability of sovereign electorates.

No doubt, these organizations have all helped, in their own way, to bring about the "moderation," and perhaps even the shrinking, of democracy. But much more efficient tools are available for the job. They take the form of debt contracts, liberally offered to populations with pressing needs for credit and with vivid dreams of a more secure life, even though these contracts create obligations and burdens that have become impossible to uphold, and intolerable to live with. Short of armed repression, the loading of debt on to all and sundry has proven to be the most reliable restraint on a free citizenry in modern times. Even if this duress were simply the unintended consequence of extending credit in the name of fair and equal access, it could hardly have served better as an instrument of social and political discipline. Taking on debt is no longer a prudent option, cheerfully sought out as a pathway to middle-class mobility and consumer comforts, as it was for a significant slice of the postwar population in the North. Indebtedness has become a general and permanent condition, experienced by most as a condition of helplessness, if not subservience.

For the masters of the art of extraction, there are two golden rules to be followed: 1) Debtors must never stop repaying, and 2) Creditors must always be made whole. Mechanisms for enforcing the first rule include: credit reporting agencies, laws tilted decisively against borrowers, creditors' powers to garnish wages and social insurance benefits, and newly revived debtors' prisons. Just as effective is the heavy-duty moralism that envelops and paralyzes the debtor who dreams of escaping the burden of debt. In a creditocracy, breaking the promise to repay is a very strong taboo. As for the duty to uphold lenders' rights, the formidable power of the financial services industry makes it more and more difficult for lawmakers not to put the creditors first. Too many elected officials are in the pockets of the major banks, and governments are so beholden to the rough justice of the bond markets that they are forced to authorize public bailouts when the big creditors seek relief, while spurning the more legitimate demands from small debtors ruined by the fallout from bankers' wild speculation.

These rules are not merely economic prescriptions, engineered to eke out maximum returns for the beneficiaries of unearned income. They are also de facto principles of governance in a *rentier* society that has roused itself, in recent decades, from its shallow Keynesian grave. The political class no longer believes it can check the royalist conduct of the bankers, even if it were capable of doing so. The banks can refuse to lend, as they have done repeatedly in the wake of the 2008 crash, but politicians cannot refuse to extend the terms of their bailout—in the U.S., the current disbursement, through quantitative easing, still amounts to $85 billion per month. As for the debtor-citizens, what is the price for our participation in this kind of society? We accept self-enforcing norms of behavior that are geared exclusively toward managing the burden of monthly payments. In a world where debt service forces us to work longer and harder in the present, and where the future is already eaten up by compound interest, the labor of imagining, let alone creating, an alternative society is easily set aside. After all, keeping the repo man from the door is already onerous enough.

To illustrate how this condition is sustained by financial "innovations," consider the technique of revolving credit, pioneered in the 1960s with the customer accounts of department stores, adopted thereafter by issuers of credit cards, and now among the most profitable vehicles of consumer lending. Under the terms of revolving credit, users appear to be in control of their own borrowing, and so they choose what they repay on a monthly basis. Credit managers, relying on judgments of "character," no longer vet borrowers or decide on their repayment schedule. The banks still set credit limits, but are all too happy to mail us a new pre-approved card when we max out (a billion and a half cards are in use in the U.S., almost five for every person). The mental trap set for revolvers is very finely conceived. For the most part, we are not aware we are actually borrowing money from the banks when we use plastic for purchases or other payments. On the one hand, payback morality demands that we try to make good on the repayments, and also that we take responsibility for the underlying behavior that triggers our failure to make minimum payments. On the other hand, the last thing that issuing banks want to see is their customers clearing their Visa and MasterCard balances at the end of each month. Bankers' profits depend on the continuous flow of merchant fees and late payment penalties and so their goal is to extend the debt service indefinitely. As users increasingly employ their credit cards to service student, medical, and housing debts, that unbroken revenue stream is a sure thing. With APRs currently around 15 percent, credit card issuers are effectively collecting $2,277 annually from the average debtor (who owes $15,185) in finance charges and penalty fees, and a much greater amount if the interest compounds daily as most now do.[3] This transfer of wealth is a consequence of debtors' desperation, yet it all proceeds in an automatic manner, and operates as if it were a form of legitimate tax collection.

Even the leeway given to users is an illusory choice. As the responsibility for paying for social needs like affordable education, shelter, and healthcare falls more and more on individuals, the private debt-financing of those basic goods is unavoidable. As the state withdraws from its obligation to make their provision affordable, the finance industry is allowed to put a series of tollbooths in place for collecting rents. The upshot of these additional fiscal burdens means that the revolving credit card has become the operational lifeline for individuals or families struggling to keep their heads above the water. They may want, or intend, to pay the monthly balance but they usually fail to make ends meet. In the banking industry, these "revolvers" in particular—numbering more than 60 percent of users—are the commercial sweet spot. They are also the ideal citizens of a creditocracy. By contrast, those who can afford to pay off the balances are known as "deadbeats," who shirk their duties because they get credit for free. There are other market segments, of course, distinguished by the status-carrying color of the cards. But by far the most sought-out customers are the long-term revolvers, as opposed to those who used to be favored because they combined "good character" with the prospect of future financial stability. Today, borrowers who diligently repay in full and have good credit scores are less desirable, though they are effectively being subsidized by the revolvers. To ensure the fullest collection of rents, a creditocracy needs a precariat with limited means to make good on its promissory obligations, and preferably one that can only ever afford partial, or minimum, payments. After all, the mathematics of compound interest determines that debts will always multiply much faster than the ability to repay them. Revolvers provide a steady stream of rents to creditors who know they can never collect in full.

This reshuffling of the merits attached to citizenly conduct is quite telling. Indeed, in the lending business, deadbeat was a label that used to be reserved for defaulters whose assets were repossessed.[4] In the kind of society that prized productivity, the promotional reward for model citizens with a strong work ethic was that they would clearly see, even if they did not always achieve, a thrift-driven pathway to upward mobility. By contrast, a society in thrall to unearned income tends to value the *chancer*, who juggles his or her credit options, consolidates loans, or borrows more to keep the wolf from the door. The more creditworthy are groomed to be revolvers in their own right, indefinitely rolling over their debts and their employment options in order to stave off bankruptcy. If these debtors are unbanked, they may be cycling through payday loans and pawnshop credit to make the minimum payments. The masters of these dodgy arts are the professional arbitrage traders at the investment banks, hedge funds, and private equity firms, strategizing (with other peoples' money) to steal a march on the markets through dicey wagers and other speculative plays.

Nor is there all that much free will attached to these newly ascendant roles. Credit card purchases yield detailed records of our daily life patterns and these are mined and analyzed to assess and further shape our data profiles as debtor-citizens. Again, the ideal is to prolong the duration of our payments and to cultivate us as lifelong debtors. If we die or actually succeed in ever paying down the principal, we are no longer serviceable. Not surprisingly, the burden of household debt is shifting toward the elderly, and even to the debt-abhorrent generation with family memories of the Great Depression. In the postwar model of life-cycle lending, it was more or less assumed that we would earn the right, in our senior years, to live debt-free, and it was a mark of pride among the elderly to have never paid a finance fee. That is no longer the case, and not just because debt-tolerant boomers are entering the ranks of the retired. On the face of it, overall U.S. household debt has decreased in the years since the 2008 financial crash. Debt service, which reached more than 14 percent of after-tax income by the end of 2007, had fallen to 10.5 percent by April 2013.[5] But that decrease was in large part the result of defaults and not repayment, as the banks have written off seriously delinquent debts. Moreover, liability has tilted disproportionately toward seniors, whose debts have increased over that same period.[6] Notwithstanding their frugal tendencies, many now have little alternative but to co-sign their children and grandchildren's loans, especially the student loans. According to the Federal Reserve Bank of New York, 2.2 million Americans aged 60 or older owed $43 billion in federal and private student loans at the end of the first quarter, up from $15 billion in 2007.[7]

Our relationship to revolving credit is often pathologized as a form of addiction, providing "debt porn" as content for reality TV-style entertainment.[8] Some users go to extreme lengths to alleviate this condition in the belief that it is primarily self-inflicted, and symptomatic of a deep character flaw. But there is no personal malady here, and least of all one that can be "cured" by getting rid of the plastic. In fact, the new social contract encourages us all to behave exactly like revolvers. Flexile overspending on a lifestyle that is always beyond our reach is a preferred mode of consumer conduct, and one that is actively courted and nurtured by the banking industry. The postwar social contract was a pact between government, capital, and labor aimed at sustaining wages and corporate profits alike. Consumer credit was extended on the basis of income growth in the future. Under the neoliberal contract, income is no longer a given, the government performs its guarantor role to the banks alone, and permanent debt is the only future certainty. The late payers who are weaned so carefully on revolving credit are more like elective role models than consumption junkies who might kick their habit if they only developed the will and the fortitude to do so.

FORFEITED RIGHTS?

Describing this condition as one of diminished citizenship is all very well, but are there any actual rights being forfeited here? Well, yes, if you consider affordable education, shelter, and healthcare as fundamental claims. More and more, access to these basic social goods is being transformed into a profit center for Wall Street, as the remnants of the welfare state devolve into what Christian Marazzi calls a "debtfare" state.[9] So, too, the right to work, which effectively rests on the affordable provision of these other requirements, is increasingly reduced to accessing the means to repay debts taken on to prepare for employability in the first place. Most balefully, the rise of a creditocracy has curtailed our right to an open future by allowing bankers so many claims on the years that lie ahead of us. Our future is mortgaged, calculated, and owned far in advance, and our democratic right to change it for the better is effectively minimized.[10]

If we evaluate the returns from political representatives, elected to uphold these rights, the results are truly meager. American lawmakers have shown that they are all but unable to protect their constituents from financial predators. In May 2009, in the immediate aftermath of the financial crash, Dick Durbin, the Democratic senator from Illinois, summed up the futility of his efforts to move his fellow legislators toward bankruptcy reform. "The banks—hard to believe in a time when we're facing a banking crisis that many of the banks created—are still the most powerful lobby on Capitol Hill. And they frankly own the place." At the time of Durbin's lament, the case for debt relief for underwater or foreclosure-threatened homeowners could not have been stronger. No less pressing was the cause of student debt relief, as an entire "lost generation" began to default in mass numbers. Yet there was no wholesale effort from the federal government to respond in an effective manner. The best offer from the Obama administration was the voluntary Home Affordable Modification Program for encouraging banks to reduce monthly payments on homeowner debt. It was set up to fail. These were the same institutions that his economic advisers had infamously bailed out to the tune of tens of trillions of Federal Reserve dollars.[11] Despite the massive federal largesse, policymakers found they had no viable means to make banks lend money, let alone reduce their own obligations. As the recession wore on, the top six banks only got bigger, controlling ever more assets, and perfecting their ability to water down even the weakest of regulatory efforts (in the form of the Dodd-Frank Act).

In the Eurozone, central banks cannot issue money to help governments close their deficits, and so the costs of the bank bailouts fell directly on taxpayers. The citizenry were further squeezed by austerity policies imposed to pay back national debt that had to be borrowed from foreign banks and bondholders. Hardest hit were the socially vulnerable populations who depend on public services that were slashed at the demand of the Troika—composed of bureaucrats from the European Commission, European Central Bank, and the IMF. In the most distressed countries, elected officials were clearly helpless, abjectly humiliated by the public demonstration of their impotence. Representative government—the seat of democratic sovereignty—was bypassed by international financial institutions with the authority to dictate economic and social policy. The Troika now acts in exactly the high-handed way that the IMF used to approach global South debtor nations—demanding cuts in health and education, public sector redundancies, reductions in the state pension, accelerated privatization of state assets (ports, utilities, land, and infrastructure), all in the name of prioritizing the repayment of foreign bondholders. Governments that accept these terms are effectively functioning as debt collectors for bondholders and banks. The outcomes are similar to those in the developing world: plummeting wages, mass unemployment, and negative economic growth, combined with rising debt burdens. The human costs are just as doleful: declining public health and life expectancy, destabilizing of communities, mounting suicide rates, and the growth of fascist loyalties.

While American federal debt is a different beast (the Federal Reserve can print money at will, and the almighty dollar is the world's reserve currency), the same formula for belt-tightening is being applied in many American cities. Municipal debt has been structured so that its costs are now routinely passed on to all of a city's residents, but especially to the most marginal populations, in the form of public payroll cuts, reneged pension promises, slashed social programs, and regressive taxation. Cut off from federal aid, starved of tax revenue, and pressured by the recession's impact to increase social service spending, local governments looking to balance their budgets are now hostage to Wall Street's ratings agencies in their desperate search for credit. In turn, Wall Street has trained its ravenous eye on the multi-trillion dollar municipal bonds industry. Hedge fund managers, who once preyed on vulnerable companies ripe for liquidation and restructuring, have turned their attention to wounded municipalities across the country. When Detroit was forced into bankruptcy in July 2013, its 12,000 public employee retirees were asked to forgo a large chunk of their pensions so that creditors like UBS and Bank of America could get repaid for dodgy derivatives transactions which had already returned handsome profits.[12] Not content with manipulating the sovereign debts of nations, predatory Wall Street lenders are now intent on capturing and looting the revenue stream of local governments. New lines of credit are opened so that cities can make their interest payments and stave off a Detroit-style default. Since all taxpayers are *de facto* participants in this municipal debt trap, none of us (not even those without personal debt) are off the hook. When representative democracy gets in the way, it is swiftly circumvented, as is the case in Detroit itself, where Kevin Orr's appointment as an "emergency financial manager" allowed him to take over full control of the city's resources from elected officials.

At every level of representative democracy, from federal legislators to city councilors, we can see the annulment of basic rights, as the claims of creditors, no matter how questionable or illegitimate, are prioritized over the needs of citizens. The specter of default, and the moralism that reinforces its civil power on behalf of the banks, is the blunt instrument with which these rights are superseded, and this power of extortion extends to the very top, as illustrated in the struggle over raising the federal debt ceiling in the fall of 2013. Indignation at the sixteen-day government shutdown further eroded trust in the ability of legislators to protect public well-being. Previously, of course, popular resistance to the usurping of democracy had become most visible through the occupations of "high-public" spaces—especially city squares like Tahrir, Syntagma, Puerta Del Sol, Paternoster, Zuccotti, and Taksim. Brutal police suppression of these encampments and related movement activism showed how far the state would go to defend the power of high finance by rooting out the effective right to public protest.[13]

It is more difficult to gauge how far the outrage traveled beyond the small multitude of *indignados* involved in the global movements of 2010-2012 or the ranks of college-educated unemployed in general. The sense of being disenfranchised is relatively new to the white middle-class majorities of the North, even the most cynical fractions among them, and so the diffusion of this mentality has been highly uneven. At one end of the spectrum are the austerity victims of the Mediterranean Eurozone, rudely stripped of their civic belongings and cast into a survivalist's netherworld. At the other end are those dispossessed of their housing surety in the foreclosure tsunami that swept through the suburban cities of California, Arizona, and Florida. In the case of the former, their attachment to citizenship is generally stronger than their self-image as consumers, and so their resentment is more directly focused on the nexus of power that allows German, French, Swiss, and Dutch bankers to ride roughshod over their national legislatures. As for those left with underwater equity in the Sunbelt states, their psychology of consumer entitlement was incubated during the long asset boom, the last rocket burn of the era of cheap credit, and, for thirty years, a hazardous substitute for falling incomes. Discomforted by being cut off from the sugary junk diet of the American Dream, their rancor is directed indiscriminately at Washington *and* Wall Street, which allows it to be diverted, by way of Tea Party ventriloquism, from the capture of the political process by high finance.

When their credit turned bad after 2008, many of these population segments woke up to find themselves in a predicament not too far removed from the debt trap imposed on populations all over the South for the last forty years. Of course, there were significant differences, primarily related to Northern complicity in centuries of colonial plunder, and especially as that history applies to the climate debts discussed in chapter five of this book. So, too, much of the white middle-class indignation is a response to being treated like the indebted brown peoples of the South, or minority populations in the North with long experience of disenfranchisement and bad debt. Even so, there is a lot to be learned from understanding the continuity between the constraints inflicted by structural adjustment policies on developing countries (from the postcolonial world to the ex-socialist periphery) and the biting austerity visited upon Northerners (from the villages of the Peloponnese to the foothill cities of the Sierra Nevada). In each case, it is impossible to separate the economic outcomes—wealth transfer to the rich—from the underlying political rationales—disciplining the hopeful, thwarting independent development and self-reliance, and, in the case of the South especially, re-binding newly emancipated masses to their former masters.

But it is just as important to acknowledge the experience of debt refusal in countries as disparate as Argentina, Russia, and

Burkina Faso. The creditors do not always get their way. Autocratic governments are especially serviceable to lenders because they can hold each citizen responsible for loans, but there is less recourse if a successor administration decides to default on debts, especially those considered to be odious. Indeed, there is an ample historical record of sovereign debt repudiation. Advocates in the Jubilee South movement in the 1990s and 2000s built a strong moral case for the cancellation of external debts, and a portion of these obligations has been cancelled through the Multilateral Debt Relief Initiative, launched at the G8's 2005 Summit in Gleneagles.

Back cover of *Tidal: Occupy Theory, Occupy Strategy*, September 2012 (courtesy R. Black)

In most cases, the argument for taking relief rested on evidence that the debts owed to Northern banks were either illegitimate or that the creditors had already been adequately repaid. In almost all cases, these obligations were outstripped by ecological debts owed by the North for five centuries of resource extraction, and for climate debts from more recent carbon emissions. So the overriding question posed by the jubilee movement—Who Owes Who?—is not simply a matter of economic accounting. To fully address the question is to assess a form of debt bondage that tethers the colonial past to the neoliberal present, and has already eaten away a large chunk of the potential for future democratic development, through debt service. If a homegrown debt resistance movement is to emerge in the North it must heed lessons from the jubilee movement launched to wipe out obligations that were unfairly imposed on the South.

IF WE REPAY, WE ARE GOING TO DIE

In the Cold War heyday, the most profitable way of using Eurodollars accumulated from aid disbursed to U.S. allies was to offer loans to developing countries. Yet just as these aid programs—the Marshall Plan (from 1948) and Mutual Security Plan (from 1951)—were aimed at stemming the spread of communism in Europe, the loans to support development in newly decolonized states were also intended to align them with the capitalist bloc of nations. This formula was vigorously reinforced by U.S. control over the multilateral agencies set up to oversee international economic relations as part of the Bretton Woods agreement at the end of the war.

The International Monetary Fund (IMF) was founded to assist countries experiencing short-term difficulties with their balance of payments. From the outset, a primary IMF agenda was to limit the rights of nation-states, previously granted by Bretton Woods, to restrict cross-border capital flows. The agenda, in other words, was to facilitate access for foreign investors to domestic markets, and its early implementation prepared the way for the hardcore promotion of free trade in the 1980s and 1990s. The World Bank was founded to make development loans that were unprofitable to private investors, though its pattern of lending, from an early point, was clearly in support of authoritarian regimes—in Portugal, South Africa, Chile, Argentina, Uruguay, Romania, the Philippines—that bent to the will of Washington.[14] The clientelist basis of the lending was further revealed when Chile was cut off during Salvador Allende's term of office, as part of Washington's "invisible blockade" of his socialist government.

The 1960s and 1970s are often referred to as the "development decades." The non-aligned movement flourished, the G77 bloc of developing nations nurtured hopes for a new international order, and self-reliance was promoted through import substitution policies and the nationalization of vital industries and resources. Large states like India, Indonesia, and Yugoslavia became standard-bearers for the promise of an independent pathway through the battle lines of the Cold War. But these dreams were being debt-financed by unscrupulous Western banks. Petrodollars, generated by OPEC oil surpluses, poured into these banks and were immediately loaned out to commodity-rich countries in the South. For Citicorp, a market leader in this business, fees and service from these loans was "the single largest source of corporate earnings through the early 1980s."[15] Yet the next several years would see massive losses from the bank's overexposure, when a wave of defaults brought the lending boom to a rude conclusion.

By the early 1980s, beginning with the "Mexican Weekend" of 1982, most of the developing world was in the grip of a debt crisis, with dozens of countries in arrears on repayment. The previous decade's dreams of autonomous development would soon dissolve under the harsh therapy prescribed by the IMF's new structural adjustment policies. The accession of India, in 1991, to the IMF's agenda of "opening up," marked the end of that aspirational era.[16] To conclude that the IMF and World Bank's orchestration of loans was directly responsible for closing the window of opportunity is not so far-fetched. Without the IMF's seal of credit approval, a country would be refused loans from all international investors, whether multilateral, bilateral, or private. But the terms for accreditation were almost as bad. The country in question had to accept the international agency's "objective" advice about how to reform its economy along lines favored by the capitalist powers. Any drift toward independence, let alone socialism, was carefully monitored and headed off. The pressure to take on the loans, along with their harsh terms, came from inside as well as from the North; domestic elites, with persuasive sway over the political class, functioned as an active fifth column.

Kleptocracy played a bigger role. Many of the loans made during the development decades were secured by dictators, and so the money ended up in their overseas accounts, held by the same banks that were making the loans. In that sense, the credit never had to travel at all. In the course of the 1970s, the aggregate debt of developing countries increased eightfold. When Federal Reserve chairman Paul Volcker unilaterally made the decision, in 1979, to raise U.S. interest rates in order to slow domestic stagflation, the cost of servicing all of those debts went through the roof. The price of raw materials plummeted, and, for many countries, the export side of their balance of payments collapsed. Facing a wave of defaults from states in the South, the IMF took advantage of their predicament to force open economic sectors that had been insulated against foreign penetration. The first structural adjustment loan was made shortly after Volcker's monetary shock therapy. Over the next two decades, these loans were the key to deregulating and privatizing the economies of even the most recalcitrant states.

Under Ronald Reagan's presidency, the Third World debt crisis was a prime opportunity to promote the policies consistent with the so-called Washington Consensus. Structural adjustment loans were offered as an emergency measure to stave off default, but they came at a staggering price to the borrower—not simply high-interest rates, but also wholesale privatization, slashed public services and government payrolls, financial deregulation, including the dismantling of import tariffs, and orientation of production away from local needs and toward foreign export markets. The medicine was most vigorously applied to countries where elected leaders had struck out on their own. Jamaica's Michael Manley was a test case. The pathway forged by his administration toward an independent version of Caribbean socialism was thwarted by a combination of IMF "stabilization" packages and a program of political destabilization aimed at replacing him with a more compliant leader—Edward Seaga, promptly nicknamed "CIAga" when he came to office in 1980.[17] Over the course of the next decade and a half, Jamaica was showcased as a paragon of free enterprise. Yet it also owed the IMF more per capita than any other country, and its overall debt burden continued to increase. When Manley himself was returned to power in 1986, he found that he was quite powerless to resist the IMF. Today, as much as 55 percent of total government spending is still being used to service Jamaica's external debt.[18]

Other leaders who were less than receptive to the IMF were pushed out of office, while those who were too compliant had to face the wrath of their people. Some met with even worse fates. Assuming the presidency of Burkina Faso after a military coup in 1983, Thomas Sankara soon proved to be one of the most outspoken resistors of the debt trap. In a memorable speech to the Organization of African Unity in Addis Ababa in July 1987, he explained how the debt crisis had been created by Northern creditors, and how they were using the crisis to further bind the South:

> "Those who lend us money are those who had colonized us before ... who used to manage our states and economies. Colonizers are those who indebted Africa through their brothers and cousins who were the lenders. We had no connections with this debt. Therefore we cannot pay for it. Debt is neo-colonialism, in which colonizers transformed themselves into "technical assistants." We should better say "technical assassins ..." Debt is a cleverly managed reconquest of Africa, aiming at subjugating its growth and development through foreign rules. Thus, each one of us becomes the financial slave—which is to say a true slave—of those who had been treacherous enough to put money in our countries with obligations for us to repay ... If we don't repay, lenders will not die. That is for sure. But if we repay, we are going to die. That is also for sure."

The charismatic Sankara was assassinated just three months later in a coup led by Blaise Compaoré, who promptly "rectified" his policies, and made amends to the IMF and World Bank. Sankara's demise was served up as a lesson to leaders who advocated Southern debtors' solidarity in the face of extortion on two fronts—from the IMF/World Bank on the outside, and from domestic elites tied to export capital on the inside. Even so, popular resistance was less easy to extinguish. Protests against the austerity delivered by structural adjustment loans—instantly labeled as "IMF riots"—spread across the South, in Peru, Egypt, Indonesia, Chile, Bolivia, Brazil, and dozens of other states, culminating in the successful revolt against water privatization in Cochabamba in 2000.[19] These insurgencies set the template for the alter-globalization movement in the 2000s, followed by a wave of European anti-austerity protests—in Lithuania, Latvia, France, Iceland, Ireland, England, Italy, Spain, and Greece—in the wake of the economic collapse, and then by the Arab Spring itself, sparked by public privation in Tunisia.

The debt crisis, which precipitated a "lost decade" of development in the South, was also an opportunity for Northern creditors to make sure they were repaid in full. Indeed, structural adjustment loans were issued on condition that the recipients prioritize repayment to the big commercial banks. The money on offer could not be used to feed, house, or educate civilians; instead the loans were approved only on condition that the creditors be made whole. This principle outlived the crisis and became an institutional norm in the decades to follow. The IMF's much-vaunted "technical advice" to borrowers increasingly consisted of lessons about how to correctly manage their loans and qualify for more credit to meet their existing debt obligations. Not much guidance was offered about how to develop their economy to meet the needs of their people, or to strengthen civil society in a freshly established democracy. Over time, debtor nations also become revolvers, borrowing from one loan installment to another simply to service interest repayments on existing debts. There was no expectation that the principal would ever be paid down, but the pattern of repayment, highly profitable in itself, had to continue uninterrupted. This principle applies today even to the IMF's Heavily Indebted Poor Countries (HIPC) initiative, launched in 1996, for countries with an unsustainable debt overhang. As Abdoulaye Wade, President of Senegal, put it, the HIPC program is "like giving aspirin to a cancer patient."[20]

In his 1987 speech, Sankara drew public attention to the Paris Club, the powerful, low-profile organization which functions as a debt collector for the creditor states, maximizing their returns, scheduling debtors' repayments, and, in some extraordinary cases, granting debt reductions for very poor nations. Along with the London Club, an even more informal institution representing private creditors, the Paris Club harmonizes and unites the power of its members. Following Fidel Castro's 1985 call for the Southern debtor nations to unite in response to the creditors, Sankara declared: "It is normal that we too have our own club—the club of Addis Ababa. It is our duty to create a unified front against debt. That is the only way to assert that refusing to repay is not an aggressive move on our part, but a fraternal move to speak the truth."

Needless to say, the Paris Club and London Club go to great pains to isolate debtors, thereby ensuring that they never act in concert. Even so, all the evidence suggests that there is almost always a payoff for debtor nations that do push back. More broadly speaking, the historical record of debt repudiation is quite a busy file. In the Americas, it stretches from the widespread defaults of U.S. states after the panics of 1837 and 1839, and again after the rollback of Reconstruction, when Southern states repudiated debts contracted by the hated "carpetbag" Republican governments, all the way to the wave of Latin American refusals from the mid-1980s onward.[21] According to Carmen Reinhart and Kenneth Rogoff, there have been at least 250 sovereign defaults on external debts since 1800, many of them the result of a disinclination to pay, as opposed to an inability to afford payments. Indeed, their survey, dating back to twelfth-century China and medieval Europe, shows that serial defaults were "an almost universal rite of passage for every country as it matured from emerging market economy to an advanced developed economy."[22]

For economists like Reinhart and Rogoff, sovereign defaults are regarded as a "serious disease," afflicting "debt-intolerant countries," and requiring a strong fiscal medicine for prevention. But for populations looking to throw off the yoke imposed by predatory foreign creditors, default and repudiation are the only rational options. Over time, moral and legal arguments have been advanced to justify nonpayment. Many of these arguments appeal to the concept of odious debt, when a new government rejects responsibility for loans taken on by a dictator or by an occupying, colonial power. For example, Cuba, acting on Washington's say-so, refused Spanish colonial debt after its independence in 1898; and in 1986, it suspended all repayments of Northern debt. The U.S.S.R. repudiated the tsar's debts, and, in turn, post-communist Russia defaulted on Soviet debts in 1998. Mindful of the toll taken by the hefty reparations bill imposed on Berlin at the Treaty of Versailles, the allies allowed postwar Germany to write off Nazi debts in 1948. Costa Rica refused its ex-dictator's debts in 1922. Other legal rationales for repudiation include fraud or corruption on the part of negotiators, coercion on the part of creditors, the transfer of private debts into public ones, and the use of loans for uses considered harmful to human and environmental rights.[23] Structural adjustment loans have also been widely regarded as illegitimate on the grounds that accepting the packages is tantamount to overriding democratic sovereignty.

In the course of the twentieth century, and especially during the Great Depression, many Central and South American countries suspended payments. In most cases, creditors ended up taking the haircuts, by agreeing to substantial reductions of outstanding debts. The same pattern played out in Argentina's monumental default in 2002, the highest-profile suspension of IMF payments in recent decades. Despite its subsequent exclusion from international finance markets, there was no long-term sanction of Argentina, and by 2005, its creditors had agreed to a 60 percent haircut. Other defaulters, such as post-Soviet Russia, were excused for geopolitical reasons, or in return for diplomatic favors. When the creditor nations want to reward countries or draw them into their sphere of influence, then the Paris Club or the London Club will oblige with a dose of debt reductions. These arrangements—in cases like Poland, Egypt, Yugoslavia, and Pakistan—are not well publicized, ostensibly to avoid encouraging moral hazard on a larger scale, but primarily out of fear that the penchant for demanding relief will spread. By contrast, lavish press coverage is sought for efforts (like the HIPC) designed to help out the most desperate debtors, in order to advertise the deep generosity of the rich nations.

According to Eric Toussaint and Damien Millet, the record shows that "an openly defiant attitude to the creditors can pay off," since those who take a firm stand usually walk away with some relief.[24] Increasingly, the repudiators stand on credible moral and legal ground. Since its founding in 1990, the Committee for the Abolition of Third World Debt (CADTM) has built up a persuasive agenda for debt cancellation, expanding far beyond the established, though still contested, legal doctrine of odious debt. A vital participant in the church-driven Jubilee 2000 movement, and an anchor of Jubilee South, which continued after 2000, CADTM holds that unilateral repudiation of illicit or illegitimate debts is not merely an option but also a responsibility of sovereign states if the debts in question violate human and environmental rights or are clearly not in the interests of the citizenry.[25]

Given the power of the banks and creditor states to skew the outcome of international arbitration, unilateral acts of refusal are considered more expedient and morally preferable. According to CATMD, cancellation is further justified if debt repayments will jeopardize the country's ability to meet basic human needs, or if creditors are aware of the harms caused by their loan packages. In some cases, *force majeure* is a consideration. For example, Paul Volcker's monetarist decision to raise interest rates in 1979 multiplied the burden of existing debts—a circumstance over which debtor nations obviously had no control. In other cases, loan rates are so high and the accompanying policy requirements so extreme that nonpayment is inevitable. Under such conditions, CADM's recommendation is that officials should regard the loans as illegitimate and subject to nullification. So, too, with debts incurred for large-scale development projects that result in undue resource exploitation and ecological harm.

Placing current debt levels in an historical context is equally important. According to CADTM data, the external debt of developing countries increased from $46 billion in 1970 to $1.35 trillion in 2007, by which time debt service on that sum had mounted to $520 billion annually ($800 billion if internal debt is included). For their part, creditors collected $460 billion more than the amount of the external loans they had offered, and that sum did not include what was left to pay.[26] Over that period of time, the debtor states had paid out $4.35 trillion in debt service (or $7.15 trillion inclusive of internal debt), repaying the equivalent of 102 times what was owed to the North in 1970.[27] In effect, the loans, on aggregate, had already been repaid. Much of the difference was a result of compound interest, banned in many societies as usurious.

An even longer view takes account of centuries of colonial extraction—of raw resources, populations lost to slavery or to forced labor, and ecological overexploitation. Any estimate of what the South owes to its Northern creditors should be weighed against this cumulative pillage, much of it absorbed into the assets of banks and investors who are in a direct line of descent from the original profiteers. The net transfer of debt wealth from South to North since 1970 is akin to the rate of extraction over similar periods during the colonial period, and the effective loss of sovereignty is comparable. If people bent on self-determination have the right to throw off the yoke of colonialism, then surely they are justified in doing the same with their debt servitude.

What civic institutions can help prepare the way for reclaiming and exercising that right? A popular referendum on debt repayment is an appropriate channel. It can be supported and informed by citizens' audits undertaken to answer questions about the conditions under which debts were incurred. Were the loans really needed? Were they properly handled? Did anyone profit personally? What were the outcomes of the loans? Did they generate public benefit? The grounds for declaring debts to be illicit or illegitimate can be laid out by a peoples' tribunal. Following an audit process provides legal support for a call for reparations or an act of cancellation. The use of referenda and audits has been pioneered in Brazil and especially in Ecuador, where the reports of the Internal Auditing Commission for Public Credit, set up in 2007, were used to back the country's bond default in 2009. The same citizens' instruments are now being pursued in debt-distressed countries in the Eurozone and North Africa.[28]

Strike Debt banner used in direct action, October 2012 (courtesy the author)

Beyond the "jubilee" phase of debt annulment lies the task of building a credit economy driven by principles of productive credit, as opposed to predatory profit. Alternative financing will be needed from credit unions and banks that have been transformed into common-interest entities. The much vaunted micro-credit programs pioneered by the Grameem Bank have only succeeded in stabilizing the ability of debtors to repay their loans. With healthy profits from interest rates that stretch as high as 100 percent in some countries, and with low default levels, it is no surprise that micro-credit is a growth business hotly courted by the big banks.[29] It remains to be seen whether the Bank of the South, founded in 2009 as a progressive alternative to the IMF/World Bank, can service the development needs of Latin American countries in a fair and functional way once it is fully operational. Yet there are cautious hopes for the cooperation of countries in a region where the spread of the Bolivarian revolution has won some autonomy from Washington. If the Latin American leftist bloc is able to sustain the unity carefully denied them by Northern creditors, it will make a historic break with the longstanding pattern of economic subjugation. In retrospect, the first step in establishing economic and political independence will have been to question and refuse the illegitimate debts owed to Northern banks and states.

DOUBLE TROUBLE IN THE NORTH

Taxpayers in the North were hardly insulated from the damage generated by the debt crisis in the South. In fact, they were carrying the banks by providing tax relief for their bad debts. Describing this subsidy as a "debt boomerang," Susan George estimated the bill as between $44 and $50 billion ("enough to meet the entire Third World's health spending for one year") during the 1980s.[30] There were other costs to be borne, but this particular technique of socializing private losses would be reprised on a much grander scale in the bank bailouts that followed the 2008 crash. Nothing prompted more rancor than the use of public funds to rescue Wall Street and Northern European banks from the debt debacles of their own making. Since most of the cost of the bailout ended up on the balance sheets of governments, the inflated deficits were subsequently used as the rationale for austerity policies. This deceptive move, described by Mark Blyth as the "biggest bait and switch of all time," was most conspicuous in Europe, where it allowed Wall Street's private banking crisis to be re-labeled as a sovereign debt crisis.[31] Harshly punished for their high debt-to-GDP ratios, the peripheral Eurozone countries, beginning with Greece, ended up being squeezed by German, French, Swiss, and Dutch banks almost as tightly as the developing countries had been over the previous three decades.

These banks, it turned out, were also badly exposed to American mortgage losses, and they had lent freely and cheaply to the peripheral states of Portugal, Ireland, Italy, Greece, and Spain, arrogantly tagged as the PIIGS. Sensing an opportunity to exploit the predicament of Greece, the most heavily indebted of these nations, predators from the hedge funds and money markets began to bet heavily in 2010 and 2011 on the prospect of Athens defaulting, or exiting from the Eurozone. The resulting run on its government bonds (Spain and Portugal were the next targets) delivered Greece further into the unyielding hands of the Troika, whose overriding goal, like that of the Paris Club, is to ensure that creditors are fully paid. In a routine exercise of self-agonizing, the IMF expressed concern at the severity of the austerity demands made on the Greek people, but no leniency was shown. At one point, the Greek premier George Papandreou was asked to submit to a deal that would have permitted private creditors to extract Greek gold from the central bank vault in the event of a default.[32] Sensing that things had gone a little too far, Papandreou refused and called instead for a national referendums on the austerity pact.

In Iceland, the decision to allow the people a voice had resulted in a refusal to repay British and Dutch creditors when the country's three high-flying banks—Kaupthing, Glitnir, and Landsbanki—failed. This spirited outcome—based on not one but two popular referenda—invalidated the Icelandic parliament's earlier decision to negotiate terms for the foreign creditors. By contrast, Greece would not be allowed to behave in such an insubordinate manner. Papandreou was pushed out of office by "the markets," the proposed referendums was shelved, and a Troika-approved technocrat, Lucas Papademos, was given the reins to ensure the smooth flow of debt repayments. In Italy, democracy also threatened to get in the way until Mario Monti, another technocrat, was appointed to exert fiscal discipline and take care of Italy's external debts. The unelected, apolitical status of these two finance industry proxies underlined the reality that the democratic process had to be suspended for the highly unpopular policies to prevail. After all, when domestic electorates vote against the fiscal wishes of the Troika, as they did in the Irish referendums that rejected the Treaty of Nice in 2001 and the Treaty of Lisbon in 2008, they are simply asked to vote again until an acceptable decision is made. Likewise, in a rare bipartisan vote in September 2008 in the U.S. House of Representatives, when Congress rejected the Troubled Asset Relief Program (TARP) $700 billion bailout of the financial industry, the barely amended bill was sent back several days later for a "correct" vote.

In the case of the Eurozone crisis, many of the banks were being bailed out twice—first in the aftermath of the crash, and then again through diverting so much of the national surplus, through austerity measures, to service the loans extended by the banks to stave off sovereign defaults. Perhaps there is one more handout in the offing, but the morality play that concealed the extortion is finally wearing thin. During the 2010-2011 Greek debt crisis, we heard no end of folderol about the superiority of the Germans' thrift and work ethic over the Mediterranean culture of sun-drenched indolence. Most of it was expressed through the litany of shame and guilt that attaches itself to the topic of debt, but always to the creditor's benefit. While this loose talk was between Europeans, it recirculated many of the figures of speech and attitudes previously applied to Third World debtor states. Irresponsible, shiftless, spendthrift, corrupt, and dependent, these populations will always need our help, but they also need fiscal discipline to make sure they can repay the financial help extended so benevolently.

Dispelling this kind of moralism is the key to pursuing the right to resist debts that cannot and should not be repaid. Counter-morality that ascribes predatory, covetous, parasitical, or sadistic behavior to the creditor is appropriate and sometimes necessary, while fact-based analysis offers credible grounds for repudiation. Contrary to the ethnic profiling of the PIIGS as pound-foolish profligates, the sovereign debts at the heart of the Eurozone crisis were not the result of public overspending. Most of these debts ballooned because of the public expense of recapitalizing banks after the crash, magnified by the impact of the hedge fund bets on government bond rates. There was barely a shred of evidence to support the call for "shared sacrifice" on the part of populations that had nothing to do with the ill-fated private speculation on short-term credit markets that brought on the recession.

Liberal economists like Robert Kuttner, Paul Krugman, and Joseph Stiglitz have argued strongly against austerity policies and for debt relief primarily on pragmatic grounds—i.e. when there is a large debt overhang, belt-tightening does nothing to promote recovery and growth. But there is a more principled and democratic response to the fraudulent act of dressing up bankers' bad bets as public debt obligations. The austerity policies themselves should be directly condemned as the result of extortion on the grounds that many of the public debts are illegitimate and therefore worthy of repudiation. In the case of Troika-imposed agreements like the much-hated 2012 Greek Memorandum, which not only overrides sovereign law but also guarantees mass impoverishment, the invocation of international human rights doctrine is a legitimate option. The UN Commission of International Law and the International Court of Hague both recognize that a state of necessity is a valid reason to retract from international obligations. Moreover, the Memorandum, which prescribed mass layoffs and pension reductions, the abolition of collective bargaining, and stepped-up privatization, was negotiated by an unelected government, appointed by the Troika and financial interests. The tactic of counter-morality is also being used to remind Germany that it has never repaid loans forcibly extracted from Greece during the Nazi occupation. Estimates of the aggregate debt, including the interest owed on the war loans, along with reparations for the Nazi damage to Greek infrastructure and stolen artifacts, are equivalent to a huge portion of the current debts owed to German creditors.[33]

In promoting such counter-claims, citizens' audits are an appropriate method for determining the inadmissibility of state, municipal, and institutional debts. Groups have sprung up in various European countries, linked through the International Citizen Debt Audit Network (ICAN), to take on this work. ICAN, whose slogan is "Don't Owe, Won't Pay," includes *Debt Justice Action* in Ireland: *Protovoulia gia tin Epitropi Logistikou Eleghou (ELE)* in Greece; *Iniciativa de Auditoria Cidadã à Divida Pública (IAC)* in Portugal; *Plataforma Auditoría Ciudadana de la Deuda* (PACD), in Spain; *Per una nuova finanza pubblica* in Italy; *Le collectif pour un audit citoyen de la dette publique* (CAC) in France; *Drop*

Egypt's Debt in Egypt; *Collectif Auditons les Créances Européennes envers la Tunisie (ACET)* in Tunisia; and the *Jubilee Debt Campaign* in the U.K. As Patrick Saurin of CAC describes it: "The goal is to look at all the public debts and decide which ones are legitimate, legal, and have a purpose that serves the public. That debt deserves to be repaid. But debts that primarily enrich banks are illegitimate and should not be repaid. The goal of the audits is to make this distinction."[34]

Citizens' audits are also a way of testing the accountability of local officials. Most municipalities and public institutions are prohibited from using public monies to speculate on the kind of toxic loan products peddled to them by banks. Indeed, the fallout from the LIBOR rate-fixing scandal has seen lawsuits against the banks by Baltimore and other cities where officials were persuaded to buy hundreds of billion dollars worth of interest-rate swaps or credit default swaps that went sour. When the outcomes of these transactions are beneficial only to the finance industry or to corrupt officials pocketing the kickbacks, there is a lawful case for non-repayment. Under these circumstances, debt audits conducted by ordinary people are also a way of promoting transparency and restoring democratic authority over common resources. Audits of local institutions with control over such resources—water and energy utilities, transportation authorities, hospitals, universities—can make ordinary people feel they are taking responsibility for reducing the yawning democratic deficits produced by the debt economy. In some cities, especially in Brazil, the audits are utilized as part of a participatory budgeting process, producing more equitable public spending.

In the case of public borrowing, the outcome of such audits is an empowering exercise in self-organization, and potentially the first step in managing these vital resources with the needs of people and not markets in mind. But can the same process be applied to household loans taken on privately as individuals? What are the grounds for repudiating these personal debts? The creditors in question are often the same ones who have manipulated sovereign and other public deficits, and extracted no end of profits through lying and cheating. What, if anything, do we owe them?

MORAL ECONOMY OF THE HOUSEHOLD

Household debts have little in common with public debts, but that hasn't stopped policymakers, especially those looking to justify austerity measures, from making comparisons between them. Barack Obama trotted out a textbook example in his 2010 State of the Union speech when he chose to announce the end of his administration's stimulus efforts and the onset of "fiscal discipline" in the form of austerity:

> "Families across the country are tightening their belts and making tough decisions. The federal government should do the same. So tonight, I'm proposing specific steps to pay for the trillion dollars that it took to rescue the economy last year. Starting in 2011, we are prepared to freeze government spending for three years ... Like any cash-strapped family, we will work within a budget to invest in what we need and sacrifice what we don't. And if I have to enforce this discipline by veto, I will."

Never mind that the comparison was groundless. No household has the Federal Reserve's power to print money—not unless one of its members is a skilled counterfeiter. Nor did Obama's rhetoric prove persuasive enough to placate the deficit scolds who had been pushing hard for an end to the stimulus and who approached the crisis in the spirit of a "shock doctrine" for reducing state provisions across the board. Fix the Debt, a lavish CEO-backed campaign that promotes "small government," relentlessly lobbied Congress to pay down the national deficit by slicing Social Security, Medicare, Medicaid, and other programs while funneling more tax breaks to corporations. One major win from the pressing of these austerians was the sequestration program, initiated in January 2013, which automatically cuts $1.5 trillion of public spending by 2020, and is an unusually cruel formula for punishing low-income populations shut out of employment and still reeling from their own version of a debt crunch.[1] The Tea Party assault that led to the government shutdown in October 2013 was aimed at making further inroads on social spending in the name of reducing the federal debt.

The resemblance Obama drew upon was misleading—governments don't have to "live within their means" in anything like the way that families do. Unlike indebted families, most of what the U.S. government owes is to itself. Like the U.K., China, and Japan, the U.S. runs on a fiat money system—the government can produce money at will. Unlike these other countries, it holds the world's reserve currency, which will always be in demand and therefore is a hedge against inflation. Unless its tax base erodes rapidly, a nation in this position ought to be able to live with high debt levels for long periods of time. In other words, the federal debt "crisis" is largely an artificial scare, cooked up to validate spending cuts that would have been politically impossible to achieve in normal circumstances. But the more subtle and insidious connection suggested by such comparisons was that lax household budgeting might also have had something to with the financial crash. In some popular accounts of the origin of the crisis, personal consumer binges, and not bankers' very risky bets, were the real cause of the collapse and the yawning federal deficit that followed in its wake. The public airing of fabrications like this helped to train moralism on the borrowing and spending patterns of American households more exclusively than was the case in Europe.

Despite all of the poisonous talk about profligate purchases of flat screen TVs and dream homes, the main reasons for the unsustainable growth of debt-financed consumption have been the rising cost of education and healthcare, combined with stagnant income. U.S. household debt-to-income levels have decreased since the peak of 177 percent in 2007, though partly as a result of mass defaults and loan write-offs. The rates of personal default, and of student debts especially, continue to climb quite steadily. Yet no serious "fix" has been proposed and no government program of personal debt write-down has emerged in response. Even from a conventional macro-economic perspective, the impact of debt deflation is alarming. Every dollar that goes to the bankers for debt service is one fewer dollar spent on goods and services in the real economy. As more and more of the surplus is extracted to increase the balance-sheet wealth of the 1 percent, the productive part of the economy has less to live on.

The Debt Boulder, deployed on the one-year anniversary of Occupy Wall Street in the Financial District, September 17, 2012 (courtesy Debt Boulder Collective)

Early on in the foreclosure crisis, distressed homeowners were counseled by voices across the political spectrum to walk away from their underwater homes. But this advice to strategically default was primarily on utilitarian grounds—there was nothing to gain, economically, from continuing to make mortgage payments. Naturally, this advice was condemned as morally irresponsible by bankers, from whom no one any longer expects ethical conduct. Other voices called for mortgage strikes, with payments going into escrow, until principal reduction was approved.[2] And some city officials, frustrated by the lack of federal action, have considered using eminent domain to buy and reduce the mortgages of underwater homeowners.[3]

Despite the massive public largesse extended to the banks, government efforts to induce them to offer reduced mortgage payment options have failed. So, too, lawsuits against Bank of America, Citigroup, JPMorgan Chase, Wells Fargo, and others for deceptive mortgage lending practices took a long time to produce outcomes for borrowers. JPMorgan's $13 billion settlement with the Justice Department in the fall of 2013 generated only $4 billion in homeowner relief. In the U.K., the fines imposed on RBS, Lloyds, Barclays, and HSBC for fraudulently selling "payment protection insurance" (PPI) were enough to generate a bump in household consumption growth. Indeed, the payouts to fleeced consumers of several thousand dollars apiece seemed to have had more of a recorded impact on the real economy than the banks' day-to-day operations. As John Lanchester wryly observed: "The banks are so bad at their primary function, lending money, that it's better for the economy if they pay billions of pounds in fines to the customers they ripped off."[4]

Aside from sporadic legal actions, most of which are settled out of court, there has been little effort, and none on a systematic basis, to determine which household debts are legitimate and which are not. But without that moral accounting we cannot begin to break the choke hold of the banks, let alone imagine a way of life without the dominion of the creditor class. Even if the government were to push through a write-down program, somehow skirting the golden requirement for creditors to be made whole, it would be for the short-term, utilitarian purpose of stimulating consumption growth and feeding the GDP. The immoral economy of debt-financing vital social goods would remain intact, and the burden on individuals would surely increase once again. Clearly, some guidelines are urgently needed to condemn this debt system as an unethical and unsustainable way of managing a society, and to move beyond it.

So where do we start? As in the case of the analysis of sovereign debts, it is important to review the underlying historical reasons for the surge in household debt. Just as with the accumulation of public debts, we will find that the growth of personal credit has been driven by an affinity for social control as much as a craving for profit. A mature creditocracy needs to satisfy both of these appetites to stiffen the will of its beneficiaries for governance.

DEALING THE BANKS IN

It took an awful long time for commercial banks to get into the business of consumer lending. For most of the period of U.S. industrialization, ample profits from their loans to business, in combination with anti-usury ceilings on interest rates, kept bankers away. Installment credit was generally made available by store owners. Because they wanted to retain their customers, in some cases no fees were charged, and so extending credit could be a losing proposition for these retailers. Middle-class individuals and families who needed loans for larger purchases relied on relatives, and immigrants turned to ethnic credit circles, while the working class had no alternative but to go to the loan shark. Bankruptcy laws, relatively late to take hold in the U.S., were designed to encourage risk-tolerance among creditors, entrepreneurs, and investors; they did not protect household debtors from the pitfalls of purchasing necessities through installment loans. Nor did usury restrictions cover borrowing for consumer goods, so rates could run high on some store credit, ruinously so in the case of the back alley sharks.

Even when usury laws were lifted in the 1920s, ostensibly to legalize personal lending and drive the sharks out of business, bankers were reluctant to jump in. It was the emergence of automobiles as a mass consumer good which dissolved any doubts about the virtues of consumer financing for large ticket items. Notably, Henry Ford held back, in deference to his strong producerist distaste for finance. His company's sales suffered when the main competitor, General Motors, forged ahead with debt-purchasing through the General Motors Acceptance Corporation (GMAC), destined to grow rapidly into a profitable arm of the corporation.[5] Subsequently, GMAC's success in wholesale and retail financing spawned imitators at other corporations, like General Electric, while independent finance companies sprang up to service the appetite for a range of consumer goods that were beyond the income reach of working families.

Competing against the appeal of socialism, prophets of consumption, like Edward Filene and Edward Bernays, promoted consumer power as an alternative to democracy in the workplace.[6] Extending credit to the masses was framed as a great act of emancipation. John Raskob, the GMAC chairman, declared that the financing efforts of firms like his would deliver "the dream haven of plenty for everyone and fair shake for all, which the socialists have pointed out to mankind. But our route will be by the capitalist road of upbuilding rather than by the socialist road of tearing down."[7] Indeed, access to credit would be a staple of the great public relations war against socialism for the next several decades, initially to ward off its influence in the U.S. and then in the worldwide contest with the Soviet bloc from the late 1940s onward.

The centerpiece of this crusade was not automobile but home ownership, the strongest pillar and most suggestive defense of Anglo-American possessive individualism against the creed of collectivism. After the 1920 Census showed a dip in homeownership, the Better Homes movement sprang up to promote the cause, beginning with the 1920 launch of "Own Your Own Home Day" by various business and civic groups as the nucleus of a National Thrift Week. In his capacity as Secretary of Commerce, from 1921 to 1928, Herbert Hoover presided over Better Homes in America, an organization formed as a hedge against irresponsible consumerism, on the one hand, and the socialist threat, on the other. Not content to simply invoke the Jeffersonian yeoman ideal of homesteading, Hoover aimed to cultivate what he called "the primal instinct in us all for home ownership."[8] In common with that ideal, the Better Homes movement assuaged public anxieties about the erosion of thrift morality in the face of the seductive appeal of market commodities. For bankers, upholding this moralism was a cover for their own self-interest. After all, personal thrift in the form of savings deposits was the basis of their own capacity to extend loans to businesses.[9]

It was not until the market promotion of house purchases was converted into a priority for national economic recovery that the commercial banks would finally be won over to the cause of consumer lending. The collapse of the housing industry in the early 1930s prompted a variety of New Deal initiatives that installed homeownership as a matter of public policy at the highest-level. The Public Works Administration (PWA) built thousands of homes, and the Home Owners Lending Corporation attacked the foreclosure crisis by directly refinancing almost one-fifth of owner-occupied homes. But it was the Federal Housing Administration (FHA) that vanquished the bankers' fears that housing was too risky to finance. The National Housing Act of 1934, which created the FHA, floated the long-term amortized mortgage along with an underlying system of government security. The insurance program would be funded by a 1 percent levy on the normative 5 percent mortgage interest rate, but it would be administered by the federal government to ensure that any defaulted loans were fully reimbursed. No public monies would be used to back the loans. The FHA's innovative use of private capital served to reassure those who saw the New Deal as a socialist plot. Indeed, one future FHA commissioner described it as "the last hope of private enterprise. The alternative was socialization of the housing industry."[10]

For banks, the icing on the cake was the creation in 1938 of the Federal National Mortgage Association (aka Fannie Mae) to trade mortgages on a secondary securities market. Lenders could now rely on nationally standardized commodity prices for selling their loans as securities, and, more important, they were able to move the loans off their books in order to make new ones. This ability to resell debts opened many doors. Bankers could now lend much more money than they possessed. (U.S. banks would attain leverage ratios of more than 35 to 1 just before the subprime mortgage crash, while European banks got up to 45 to 1—the ratio of Barclays' assets to its equity was 61.3 to 1 at its 2008 peak.)[11] Debts could be borrowed against as if they were assets, especially if they were federally guaranteed, the responsibility for bad loans could be passed on to whoever was unfortunate enough to buy them, and the government would take care of the administrative costs through Fannie Mae (an arrangement reprised later, for student debt, through Sallie Mae). As long as the system was well regulated it was a stable arrangement, producing steady profit in an era of rising incomes. But deregulation over time meant that the resale of these housing loans, especially the "nonconforming," or subprime, ones, spawned a towering pyramid of debt instruments and speculative bets in the form of derivatives, highly susceptible to systemic collapse.

Neutralizing the risk for bankers became a habit of government, but it came at a high cost, and the price was paid repeatedly by taxpayers, beginning with the bill from the savings and loans crisis of the 1980s. Estimated at $370 billion, this tab would be dwarfed by the trillions of dollars' worth of fiscal damage after 2008. The ballooning cost of these bailouts was a direct consequence of the New Deal pact with government that Wall Street was all too happy to keep alive. Despite the federal obligation to absorb the banks' risks, there was little reciprocity in that relationship. When the large banks were rescued from insolvency after 2008, Congress lacked the power to make them restart lending, even to each other. Many commentators concluded that the legislators' reins of regulation had simply worn too thin to do the job, but some part of the structural weakness was due to the sweetheart deal that got the banks into consumer credit in the first place.

The lending standards approved by the FHA and Fannie Mae were the architectural foundation of the long postwar consumer boom. The FHA-insured suburban home was a container to be filled with goods purchased at department stores on Charga-Plate (a predecessor to the credit card), and then through option accounts, and finally on the basis of revolving credit. In this period, the full rights of citizenship were reserved for those who had entered into a long-term debtor relationship with a commercial bank. For those who qualified—predominantly white suburban home purchasers—the default rates were low. With economic growth steady, and rising incomes assured, uninterrupted monthly payments were almost guaranteed. Even so, the fear of a damaged credit score, or threat of a foreclosure, helped to reinforce the rigid status quo that was so distinctive of the Cold War culture of conformity. Debt service was the key to enforcing social norms, and so the mortgaged home became the cornerstone of capitalist ideology in this period. As William Levitt, the masterbuilder of mass suburban homes, so concisely put it, "No man who owns his own house and lot can be a communist."[12] Even so, he was simply expressing an opinion that, for twenty years, had guided a generation of urban planners, like John Nolen, and housing reformers, like Lawrence Veiller, in their bid to foster "a conservative point of view in the working man."[13]

Making credit available for home purchases was one thing; ensuring a well-housed citizenry was another. The "right of every family to a decent home" had featured prominently in FDR's 1944 economic bill of rights, and the 1948 Housing Act promised a "decent home in a suitable living environment for every American." But there was a notable decline in official U.S. political support for the right to housing from the 1960s.[14] In 1996, in response to pressure from human rights advocates, the State Department asserted that it "must make clear for the record that the U.S. does not recognize the international right to housing," and that it preferred a weaker recognition that decent housing is simply an ideal to be pursued.[15] By that time, the right to access credit, and thereby join the ranks of long-term debtors, had long supplanted the right to housing, just as the right to education was giving way to the right to access student loans.

Redlining, deed restrictions, and racial covenants meant that only white male borrowers qualified for the low-interest FHA loans; minorities and single women had to pay much more for homeownership and for all kinds of credit, which made them easier prey for scammers. Well into the 1970s, installment credit was still the retail norm in minority-dominated urban areas, where storeowners kept customers' debt ledgers as they had done since the early days of the republic. David Caplowitz's landmark 1967 study, *The Poor Pay More,* showed that low-income urbanites were being charged more in their neighborhood stores for the same goods sold to middle-class consumers in suburban department stores. Since they only had credit with the local retailers, they could not comparison-shop, and so became a captive, and easily exploited, market. Repossession of furniture and other household goods was still a common occurrence, amplifying, as neighbors looked on, the debtor's shame. It was no surprise that much of the anger incited by the urban riots of the 1960s was directed against retail stores owned by white outsiders. The spectacle of "looting" was played up in the mass media. But from another perspective, lifting appliances from stores was simply an act of debt-free consumption at the cost of retailers who had bled their customers dry. In a sense, the goods had already been paid for, from years of usury and extortion that accompanied installment debt. Hence the widespread rumors that the store owners' credit records were burned before the merchandise was taken.[16]

CITIZENSHIP IN THE DEBTORS' REPUBLIC

The riots produced a lot of hand-wringing on Capitol Hill, and, in due time, a token share of new programs and services to the urban poor. But what emerged as a long-term legislative principle was the need to broaden credit access to the excluded, who were still falling victim to predatory lenders. Low-income African Americans were foremost among them, but, since credit scoring was based entirely on the life patterns of males, even middle-class white women were unable to secure loans at reasonable rates. Congress subsequently passed a series of bills—the Consumer Credit Protection Act in 1968, the Fair Credit Reporting Act in 1970, and the Equal Credit Opportunity Act in 1974—which tried to introduce uniformity in credit transactions and banned discrimination on the basis of race, gender, religion, national origin, and age. The legislation was aimed at a level playing field, but it also further institutionalized the idea that first-class citizenship was only to be attained through going into debt. Rather than more fully realize the right to basic social goods, like healthcare, education, and housing, what was upheld was the right to privately debt-finance these goods—a right, in other words, for which creditors had to be paid with debt money.

For the burgeoning financial services industry, this was the only form of civil rights that mattered.

Compared to the state-guaranteed public provision of social goods, the ability of individuals to fund them on a private basis was neither secure nor stable. It depended either on steadily rising incomes or appreciating asset values. When wages in the U.S. stagnated in the 1970s, overall household debt shot up. From then on, maintaining living standards was only possible through the profits from resale of property—every seven years for the average American homeowner. The American Dream was achieved not through buying a home, but from selling it at a higher price. The "consumers' republic" of the postwar years, as described by historian Lizabeth Cohen, extended the promise of full democratic participation in the marketplace of commodities, and was upheld by lofty political rhetoric about freedom from want.[17] The consumers' republic did not always deliver on its promise, not even to the white suburbanites it favored most, but when income growth stalled, it segued into a "debtors' republic". In this more lopsided version of the equal participation society, the banks were the ones enjoying full access to a marketplace of credit built around the desperate efforts of consumers to keep up with the costs of their aspirations.

Each uptick in the levels of desperation brought new promotions of financial products designed to exploit the predicaments of households on the ropes. As medical and college tuition bills mounted, homeowners had to be allowed to borrow more against the collateral of their houses. Home equity lines of credit (HELOCs) became a particularly popular option in the 2000s. A HELOC is a line of revolving credit with an adjustable interest rate, which allows the borrower to choose when and how often to borrow up to an agreed limit. As for a credit card, the minimum monthly payment can be as low as only the interest that is due. Before long, borrowers were being encouraged by banks to treat HELOCs like an ATM machine or a credit card, by using them to service their own Visa and MasterCard debts. Few of these loans—liberally extended during the subprime era—were used for their avowed purpose of home improvement. Such was the perverse nature of the debt trap that tightened its grip around households in the run-up to the financial collapse. In the wake of the housing crash, the seemingly indiscriminate use of these home equity loans was often portrayed as profligacy on the part of people who were clearly living beyond their means. Playing up their lack of self-restraint was a way of pinning sole responsibility on debtors for the bankers' own choice to make risky loans. Needless to say, moralizing along those lines belonged to a long tradition of blaming the victim for a predicament designed and manipulated by creditors who aggressively marketed the loans and then sold on the risks.

Redirecting the moral scrutiny at the avarice of lenders gives a more accurate picture of the quandary that led to the massive levels of household debt attained on the brink of the 2008 crash. By late 2007, U.S. household debts had risen to 130 percent of after-tax income.[18] This overall debt had grown from nearly zero in the 1950s to its peak of $13.8 trillion just before the crash, and the most precipitous rise occurred from 1980 to 2008, when household debt rose from 43 percent to 97 percent of GDP.[19] This steady increase in borrowing is hardly surprising, given that the median family income has barely budged since 1973. But consider where the wealth has gone during that same period of time. The highest-earning 1 percent took more than 60 percent of all income gains between 1979 and 2007, and more than 95 percent since 2008.[20] By far the largest part of this wealth was generated from the financial manipulation of debt—and much of it from force-feeding customers with cheap credit. In the decade before 2008, the average American household was handing over almost one in every five dollars of after-tax income to Wall Street in debt service.[21] Those ratios have decreased somewhat in the last five years, largely because of low interest rates, and also because the banks have written off so many "nonperforming" loans, but they are expected to shoot up when interest rates increase.

Any honest analysis of this vast transfer of wealth shows who benefitted royally from the accumulation of household debt over the last thirty years. Whose lack of self-restraint placed a crushing burden on the population at large? Who exhibited rent-seeking conduct that was predatory in nature? Do they really deserve more debt service after decades of stripping wealth from borrowers? Can we not conclude that they have already been repaid many times over?

From a banker's perspective, any consumer good or asset is simply a vehicle for raking in debt payments—the collection of interest, fees, penalties, and commissions is all that matters. But the interest on, say, a 5 percent FHA loan is small potatoes compared to the revenue from speculative bets on the performance of securities based on such loans. The creation of mortgage-backed securities—typically a pool of housing loans packaged and sold like bonds to investors—was the key to these exploding profits. Ginnie Mae (the Government National Mortgage Association), created to increase the nation's affordable housing stock by tapping capital markets, issued the first mortgage-backed securities in February 1970 as part of a pitch to employee pension funds. The sale of these government-backed bonds was intended to create capital for cheap loans to low-income home buyers, but it opened the door to a whole new world of securitized loans in which lenders could offload their responsibilities onto investors with no connection to the borrowers. Reinvesting capital from selling a loan proved much more lucrative than patiently collecting returns from it.

When derivatives in the form of CMOs (collateralized mortgage obligations) were introduced as speculators' bets on how the asset might perform over time, the formation of profit was even further removed from the original lender-borrower relationship. The original lender was only the first in line to pass on the risk of default. The risk (and quarantining of losses) was distributed far and wide, generating fees along the way for investment bankers, lawyers, brokers, and credit agencies, among others. Eventually this long line of *rentiers* would be joined by issuers of the multitudinous credit default swaps intended to insure against defaults. Under those circumstances, there was every incentive to make the kind of subprime or NINJA (No Income No Job No Asset) loans that could never be repaid, and that lay at the toxic heart of the financial crash. Creditors who make such loans knowingly have no reason to expect they will ever be repaid. But the loans will have "performed" well enough for those who take their cut along the great chain of risk redistribution.

Housing debt was only the first kind of loan product to be securitized in this way. Student and auto loans were next, followed by contracts like equipment and aircraft leases, and then life and catastrophe insurance. Every kind of contractual debt could be pooled and transformed into a market trade, but arguably the most significant was credit card debt, first securitized in 1986, and now the largest sector (21 percent) of the market. Through securitization and other "financial innovations," very few of which serve any social purpose at all, Wall Street has come up with thousands of new ways to extract economic rents. Among the most durable was the creation of revolving credit, which evolved from the thirty-day credit option accounts that retailers offered customers in the 1950s. Instead of being required to clear the balance every month, the new arrangement allowed consumers, especially those with irregular cash flow, to choose their own repayment schedules, generating huge fees and penalties as a result. Revolving credit was a recipe for perpetual debt, and it proved immensely profitable, transforming the risk of mass default into a secure source of revenue for creditors.

The Supreme Court's *Marquette* decision in 1986 effectively voided the state usury laws that had made it unprofitable to lend to likely defaulters. After *Marquette's* ruling that interstate loans were governed by a bank's home state and not by the borrower's location, credit card firms rushed to relocate to states without rate caps, like Delaware and South Dakota. Subsequently, most other states removed their usury caps in order to stem the exodus. The other big boost to bank profits was the advent of credit card securitization in 1986. Moving credit card debt off their books allowed banks to capitalize ever more loans, indeed as many as they wanted. The risk was passed on to capital markets, along with any need to secure the debts.

Hidden fees were added and late payment penalties were hiked, as banks discovered just how much money could be made from revolvers. The successive waves of blue-collar and white-collar layoffs in the 1980s brought millions of new customers into the revolving market. As these workers slid out of the middle class, plastic was their only cushion. When holes in the social safety net appeared, seniors were also persuaded to ease up on their traditional resistance to carrying long-term personal debt and were duly recruited to the revolver ranks. Not surprisingly, the explosion in credit card profitability propelled banks to seek out ever more marginal customers: the working poor, the unbanked, college freshmen, even high school students. These subprime populations were risky by any historical standards of creditworthiness, but they were sought out as likely revolvers. Aggressively plied with "kiddie cards," the younger ones were especially prized as lifelong captives. As with every profile of debt, racialization proved to be a factor. African American and Latin@ cardholders are much more likely than whites or Asian Americans to miss payments and to become dependable revolvers. As for the "convenience" users who can afford to pay on time, they are enjoying what banks see as "free credit," but only at the expense of the subsidy provided by revolvers.

Consistent with Caplowitz's principle that the poor pay more, the unbanked (as much as 12 percent of the U.S. population, while one in five households are defined as underbanked) are the most systematically exploited in their search for credit. Populations who cannot afford, or who do not qualify for, accounts at accredited banks are forced to use alternative or "fringe" lenders whose storefront outlets abound in low-income neighborhoods. These are creditors who prey on the working poor through services that include check cashing, rent-to-own finance, auto title lending, refund anticipation loans, pawnshops, prepaid credit cards, and payday loans.[22] Some of these forms of credit carry astronomical rates of interest—a typical payday loan will charge an annual rate of between 390 percent and 550 percent, while online lenders can extract from 800 to 1000 percent interest annually. Payday loan stores were virtually unheard of in the 1980s. Now there are more in the U.S. than McDonald's restaurants, and they are concentrated in low-income minority neighborhoods, though, as the economy worsens, they are cropping up on Main Street and in the strip malls of middle-class suburbia. In Eurozone cities under the hammer of austerity, like Athens, pawnshops have entered the retail mix of prime shopping thoroughfares.

While these credit-gouging "poverty banks" proliferated during the 1990s era of deregulation, their business practices hark back to the loan sharks of pre-Fordist era, and each has engineered ways to circumvent usury laws. Since renting, for example, is not considered borrowing, the use of virtually any good can be financed at usurious rates if it is advertised as rent-to-own. Indeed, the latest growth sector in fringe finance is the rent-to-own tire business, obliging customers to pay three or four times the retail price over the duration of a contract.[23] Taken as an industry, fringe financial services collectively extract $2,500 on average in debt service from each of the forty million households in the U.S. with incomes less than $30,000 a year. On after-tax incomes, this amounts to a 10 percent annual "poverty tax," according to Gary Rivlin, which is a massive surcharge on those without access to prime services.[24] These are among the poorest people in the U.S.—too poor to borrow from anyone else—yet the profits sucked out of them are typically greater in proportion to their income than the debt repayments extracted by Citibank or Bank of America from their qualified middle-class customers.

Not surprisingly, and for the same reasons they are drawn to micro-lending in the South, the big Wall Street players are increasingly involved in fringe finance, even though their names are not on the storefronts. In fact, some operations are joint ventures with the majors. More than 40 percent of the payday loan industry enjoys lines of credit with major banks like Wells Fargo, JPMorgan Chase, US Bancorp, and Bank of America, which means that lenders can borrow money at 2.5 percent APR and sell loans at 500 percent. Borrowers fork over more than $3.4 billion per year in payday loan fee payments, and, overall, $3.1 billion in profits is stripped annually from their pockets.[25] Rivlin estimates that $30 billion in fee payments flows through alternative fringe services as a whole. It is easy to see why the creditors, whether they are too-big-to-fail banks, or mom-and-pop storefront operators, love the poverty business. Contrary to those who believe that indebtedness is a middle-class problem, relevant only to those who can afford homes and a college education, the dependence of low-income families on Loan Alley is a baleful condition, evocative of the debt peonage of centuries ago.

The ideal customers of fringe finance are repeat borrowers, and, once again, they closely resemble credit card revolvers. Unable to clear their debts, they are expected to make minimum interest payments, and are often in the market for new credit to help clear these payments or make a dent in the older loans. Given the exorbitant rates, and the variety of scams imposed on their customers, the sector as a whole gets paid back handsomely as the borrower's debt increases. A society that allows these lending practices to flourish is one that sanctions not only extortion, but also wage theft. After all, check cashing outlets flourish on the premise that workers must hand over a percentage of their labor compensation simply in order to access them. Banks, eager to capture these fees, have begun to persuade large corporations like Walmart, Home Depot, Walgreens, Taco Bell, and McDonald's to pay their employees with prepaid debit cards that are only lightly regulated. The card providers charge the user fees to make ATM withdrawals and retail purchases, along with inactivity fees for not using their cards. Almost all of these are minimum or sub-minimum wage employees, compelled to fork over a fee to enjoy their paycheck.[26]

One hundred years ago, commercial banks shunned personal lending to the creditworthy middle-class, never mind working families in the same income bracket as these Walmart employees. Since that time, consumer credit has become the most profitable of all finance sectors. Those living from paycheck to paycheck, or even failing to do so, are no longer ignored—they are now targeted as sources of high revenue. The flow of payments from the most penurious members of society contributes disproportionately to the ongoing net transfer of wealth to the top-income echelons. When the flow is threatened, the police, increasingly, intervene. A third of U.S. states now jail people for not paying off their debts, even for minor infractions like traffic fines, and some apply surcharges, collection fees, and additional "poverty penalties" through the court system. This resurgent form of the old debtors' prison, outlawed in the 1840s, is tantamount to criminalizing poverty.[27]

How do these "crimes of poverty" compare to the serial malfeasance of financial firms, whose fraudulent schemes (hawking junk loans to all and sundry, robo-signing foreclosure documents, the PPI scandal, manipulating the LIBOR rates, and then manipulating the prices of interest-rate swaps, to name only the most widely publicized) continue to generate headlines but very little in the way of criminal prosecutions or regulatory action? [28] The executives of the "too big to fail" banks are not only too big to jail; the power they exert over policymaking allows them to collect capital gains at undertaxed rates, and tax-free interest on margin loans used to purchase paper claims. The Bank of America, the nation's largest, paid no federal taxes in 2010, and actually took in a $1.9 billion IRS rebate, but it was the recipient of $1.34 trillion from the Federal Reserve as part of the 2008 bailout. Citigroup, once the world's largest financial firm, has managed to pay no federal income taxes for the last four years, but it received a total of $2.5 trillion in financial assistance from the Federal Reserve.[29] Nor are the bailouts over. The Federal Reserve is still serving as a bad bank, buying up worthless mortgage-backed securities that were triple A-rated by the agencies that aided and abetted the pre-2008 asset boom. Estimates of the overall Federal Reserve tally for the bank bailout vary quite widely, but one calculation, from November 2011, put the total at a mind-boggling $29.5 trillion.[30]

This is the cost of protecting those who cheat and lie, who prey upon the working poor, and who bribe officials to assist their efforts to loot the common wealth. What do we call a democracy when its political class cannot check the outlaw power of the creditor class in this way, but locks up its neediest citizens when they cannot pay their water bills?

FAILED DEMOCRACY?

Anyone can spot the conventional indicators of a failing democracy. An elected government suspends guarantees such as free speech, privacy, or habeas corpus, usually citing some shadowy foreign threat. Persons are held and imprisoned without specific charges, police agencies are empowered to wiretap and search at will, and daily life becomes increasingly militarized. These measures are easier to detect in countries far removed from our own. Yet since 9/11, the U.S. has traveled quite far down that road, with the upholding of the Patriot Act provisions, the institutional growth of "homeland security," the overreach of the 2012 National Defense Authorization Act, the emergence of a vigorous foreign policy of extrajudicial assassinations, and the mass citizen surveillance programs of the National Security Agency.[31]

Another sign of a failed democracy is when a supranational body is allowed to bypass the power of an elected government in order to dictate policy, either directly or through setting terms that drastically limit the available choices. Most recently, sovereign debt crises have placed several Eurozone nations in this quandary; they are currently under the "tutelage" of the Troika, as many developing countries before them were subject to the IMF's discipline. Global-justice advocates in the 2000s saw the World Trade Organization in the same undemocratic light. An unelected body structured to favor corporate-driven globalization, it undermined national sovereignty by imposing trade rules on populations to whom it was beyond accountability.[32]

No less broken is a democracy, like the U.S., in which financial elites are allowed to hold citizens in near-servitude through debts contracted for the basic requirements of life. Under these circumstances, household debt so constrains the majority that their life choices are minimized, and they feel their futures have been foreclosed. The monopoly of creditors extends beyond the realm of economic extraction to tight political control over lawmakers, all but voiding their capacity to protect the citizenry from harm. Historically, the power of creditors to make these kinds of unchecked demands on the population at large led directly to peonage and slavery. Ancient societies, in Sumer, Babylon, and Egypt, resolved the problem by royal fiat in the form of a jubilee, or periodic debt cancellation through "clean slate" decrees, whereby slaves were freed and property seized by creditors was returned to its original owners.[33]

In the jubilee tradition, freedom from debt bondage is an aspiration intrinsically bound up in the ideal of citizenship. This is one of the reasons why societies have chosen to ban usury, whether through religious proscription or as matter of civil, even natural, law. Such bans range from outright interdictions on lending money at interest to rate capping and prohibition of compound interest. [34] Islamic banking prohibits usury (*riba*) and sanctions "ethical" investments that are consistent with the principles of *sharia*. The Christian jubilee tradition has focused mostly on the remission of sins. But in the lead-up to the Great Jubilee year of 2000, the campaign for Southern debt abolition, conducted by a global coalition of churches and other civil society organizations, was directly tied to Catholic anti-poverty doctrine and was formally supported by Pope John Paul II. Other jubilee organizations continued the campaign to "drop the debt" after Jubilee 2000 dissolved, and extracted a significant degree of debt cancellation from the G8 countries, though many of the promises remain unfulfilled.

In the U.S., the foremost example of the jubilee tradition was the Emancipation Proclamation of 1863. The great "trump of jubilee," as Frederick Douglas described it, is still celebrated by many African American communities on January 1st as Jubilee Day. Yet when Reconstruction in the South was rolled back after 1877, the promise of yeomanry for freed slaves gave way (as it often has done after a break from serfdom) to a neo-feudal order of perpetual debt servitude under tenant farming and sharecropping. Ambrose Bierce's *Devil's Dictionary*, written at that time, contains the following definition: "Debt. n. An ingenious substitute for the chain and whip of the slave-driver." Likewise, the momentous civil rights reforms of the 1960s have been followed by a mercurial growth in the incarceration of African Americans. Today's increasingly for-profit prisons are crammed full of black males unjustly forced to "pay their debt to society." Serving time does not dissolve the debt, moreover, since felons, in direct line of descent from the days of slavery, convict leasing, and Jim Crow, are permanently denied basic civil and human rights.[35]

Governments that are powerless to prevent the growth of a carceral state or the onset of debt bondage are also too weak to follow through fully on their guarantee to creditors that citizens will be responsible for public debts. Creditors looking to squeeze out every last cent of debt service have no alternative but to use enforcers like the IMF to override the sovereignty of democratic process and impose austerity measures on highly unpopular terms. In taking this route, the financial oligarchs risk losing the state's capacity to maintain political control on their behalf (rule by consent is a more effective form of oligarchy than rule by coercion), and so populist protest and deepening class conflict is almost certain to follow. At that point, the choices for any democracy become quite stark. The power of bondholders to forcibly extract payments is pitted directly against popular self-determination.

On one side of this face-off is the creditor class, mustering all the weapons of contract law and payback morality against the citizenry of the debtor nation, piling on charges of laziness, benefit fraud, tax avoidance, or, in the softer version, calling for "shared sacrifice" from all. Its loyal economist allies trot out research to give substance to the moralizing. For example, policymakers may be warned that high "debt-to-GDP ratios" will generate negative growth, as Carmen Reinhart and Kenneth Rogoff did in their influential 2010 argument for ending the Keynesian fiscal stimulus measures adopted by many countries after the 2008 crash.[36] By the time their argument was discredited, in April 2013, as the outcome of a spreadsheet error, the damage to national systems of social insurance, welfare spending, and collective bargaining rights had been done.[37] The austerians lost some of their intellectual credibility—Reinhart and Rogoff dismissed the error as an "academic kerfuffle"—but their policies had already been widely implemented, spreading immiseration and despair among populations with the least resources.[38]

On the other side are the active citizenry, who see no reason to trust that elected officials can respond to their grievances, let alone act on their behalf. Instead, many begin to practice their own forms of "real democracy" through public assembly, and by pioneering direct action and alternative ways of getting things done, such as mutual aid or commoning. These responses are a consistent thread running through the new movements—from the insurgencies in Tunisia and Egypt, and the encampments of 15M, Syntagma, and Occupy, to the mass mobilizations in Turkey and Brazil. Representative democracy seems to have lost its appeal, or its right to demand prior allegiance from participants in these movements.[39] While the grievances expressed by the throngs in the squares were manyfold, the refusal of illegitimate financial debt often emerged as a common or unifying element. Indeed, the most ubiquitous street slogans spoke directly to the asymmetrical treatment of creditors and debtors—"We Won't Pay For Your Crisis" (a familiar refrain in Europe) and "Banks Got Bailed Out, We Got Sold Out" (the marching chant of Occupy Wall Street).

Strike Debt logo (courtesy MTL)

For many of the protesters, the sharpening conflict between creditor and debtor is more meaningful than the traditional struggle between capital and labor. Their crusading goals, for the most part, are not full employment, nonalienated work, bargaining rights, and decent benefits, though these have hardly been superseded, and are still central to the anti-precarity movement groups. But capital owners in pursuit of profit have long moved beyond the workplace and into the "social factory" of everyday life.

Their extractive reach now touches each daily activity, and so exploitation through personal debt encroaches on every aspect of selfhood. As such, the debt burden is felt more intimately than workplace exploitation, if only because it cannot be cordoned off as the contractual time we owe to our employers. Since the extraction is experienced as an existential threat, close to the constitutional bones of life and liberty, the impulse to cast off the bonds of debt is all the more tangible to people as an act of self-empowerment. When that impulse takes a collective form, it can muster a broad alliance with a formidable moral appeal.

Restoring the moral economy of the household can take many paths. At one end of the spectrum we might find the principle of setting a fair price for social goods, as opposed to "whatever the market can bear." At the other end would be efforts to replace the logic of market transactions with ones based on cooperative and mutual aid networks. What would a similar spectrum of positions on debt annulment look like? At one end are the advocates of writing down debts to reflect the ability to pay. *El Barzon*, the middle-class debtors movement that emerged in Mexico after the devaluation of the peso, adopted this position, as summarized by their motto: "*Debo, no niego, pago lo justo*" ("I owe, I don't deny it, I'll pay what is fair"). At the other end are those who favor the clean slate of the jubilee, or who reject most debts as illegitimate. But the first step is to decide how to topple the boulder of debt from our backs. What follows are some principles and arguments—many have been mentioned previously in passing—to help dislodge the burden.

Making loans that clearly can never be repaid in full is a more delinquent act than being unable to pay. Making a killing off vital common goods like education and healthcare and public infrastructure is venal, anti-social conduct, to be condemned and not indemnified. The money we borrowed from banks was not theirs to begin with—it was created as interest-bearing debt, only when we signed the loan agreement. The long record of fraud and deceit on the part of bankers disqualifies their right to be made whole—it is more moral to deny them than to pay them back. The banks, and their beneficiaries, awash in bonuses, profits, and dividends, have already been paid enough. Since the creditor class produces phony wealth, fake growth, and thus no lasting prosperity to society as a whole, it deserves nothing from us in return. Loading debt onto the citizenry inflicts grievous damage on any democracy, no matter how durable it appears to be. When a government cannot—or will not—respond, then taking debt relief for ourselves, by any means necessary, may be the most indispensable act of civil disobedience. Asserting the moral right to repudiate debt may be the only way of rebuilding popular democracy.

What lies beyond immediate debt relief? The hard task of building a successor economy around the principles of socially productive credit, as opposed to one run on predatory debt. For as long as Wall Street draws its strongest profits from trading derivatives built around dodgy consumer loans, selling the associated risks, and multiplying its own assets through the "miracle" of leveraging, banks have no incentive to make investments in tangible goods or productive enterprise that might create jobs, income, taxes, and thereby generate public benefits. When hedge funds rake in cash by exploiting differences in market prices, when investment banks profit from transactions on purely financial bets, or when commercial banks issue credit to consumers simply to assist with existing debt service, the fantasy of money creating more money is tantalizingly close at hand.

The dream of realizing some of this phony wealth was extended to all in the course of the pre-2008 credit bubble. Now we know that Wall Street's mathematically complex methods for dispersing risks turned out to rest on one simple principle—the ultimate underwriter of these risks would be the taxpayer. The bills are still arriving on our laps, whether directly, or having passed through the austerity-generating filter of public debt en route. But the final leg of this cycle is the cruelest, because the bills can only be paid by taking on more household debt. That is why it is a recipe for future debt peonage. Our governments are not in a position to break that cycle. They have had five years to do it, and the power of the banking giants has only grown. The task of breaking the bonds of debt is for us to take on, and it is the all-important step toward forging new social bonds among ourselves.

The financial bonds, we are often told, are too knotty to untie, because the relationship between household debtors and creditors has become more and more indirect. Every kind of personal debt—whether medical, student, housing, or credit card—is now sold, securitized, and collateralized. As a result, overleveraged streams of interest and principal can end up anywhere, owned by *rentiers* many times removed from the original lender and the real underlying assets. Thanks to the practice of drawing pension funds into the finance marketplace, workers themselves have become *de facto* creditors—and so the line between creditors and debtors, we are told, has become too blurred. Through securitization and derivatives, Wall Street has created what Robert Kuttner calls a "doomsday machine"; even if we wanted to cancel housing debt, it may be a "legal and logistical impossibility," he argues, to turn mortgages back into their original form.[40] It turns out that Wall Street's academically gifted "quants," the "best minds of their generation" who flocked to work for Goldman Sachs, Lehman Brothers, and Merrill Lynch, could only take apart contracts, they could not put them back together into formats that reflected recognizable human relationships.

It's all too plain that this debt-money system without accountability was not created, nor is it maintained, for our common welfare. Its web of obligations does not serve the vast majority who are forced to borrow for basic needs, and we know it is constantly being re-engineered to trap us ever more tightly in its threads. To the degree to which a creditocracy provides little benefit to us or to society as a whole, perhaps we should decide that we owe its real beneficiaries nothing at all.

EDUCATION FOR FREE PEOPLE

Plainly alarmed by the growth and deepening of civic activism over the course of the previous decade, the authors of the 1975 Trilateral Commission report, *The Crisis of Democracy,* recommended that "the effective operation of a democratic political system usually requires some measure of apathy and noninvolvement on the part of some individuals and groups." Given the prominent role that student protest had lately played in plaguing the political establishment, it was no surprise that the college-educated population, which had surged in the wake of the GI Bill and the 1965 Higher Education Act, merited special attention. Weighing the reasons why these college types had become less apathetic than was good for democracy, the authors lamented "the overproduction of people with university education in relation to the jobs available for them," and, in the conclusion to the report, posed two options:

> "Should a college education be provided generally because of its contribution to the overall cultural level of the populace

> and its possible relation to the constructive discharge of the responsibilities of citizenship? If this question is answered in the affirmative, a program is then necessary to lower the job expectations of those who receive a college education. If the question is answered in the negative, then higher educational institutions should be induced to redesign their programs so as to be geared to the patterns of economic development and future job opportunities.[1]"

Readers may differ on which path has been followed more decisively in the decades since, but it is impossible, today, to consider these options without looking into the deepening abyss of the student debt crisis. Any discussion about the virtues or purposes of higher education is now weighed down with the grim cargo of accumulated debt, its debilitating toll on young people, and the apparent immunity of those who feed off their predicament. A system that has run up close to $1.2 trillion in cumulative debt, and that spits out graduates with a debt load averaging $27,000, was unimaginable in 1975, when public support for higher education was still a high national priority. And yet, in retrospect, the downslope was just around the corner. That same year, New York City was caught in a fiscal crisis, which would result in the termination of free tuition at the great working-class institution of CUNY. Fees at the nominally free University of California, which aspired to be the world's model public university, began their steady ascent a few years later.

Campus protest is no longer a rite of passage as it was for most students in the 1960s and 1970s. Has the rising debt burden helped to stifle the optional political imagination of students in the ensuing decades? Can it be blamed for restoring the "apathy and noninvolvement" recommended to the Trilateral Commission as a cure for the "excess of democracy"? American students today are typically handed out hefty loan packages on enrollment, long before they are legally allowed to drink alcohol; many are compelled to seek out low-pay jobs to stay in college and stave off further debt; they are encouraged to think of their degree as a transaction in which their future wages have been traded; and they are increasingly directed toward fields of study that provide "value" through the earning potential to repay their loans. These are not conditions under which an agile critical mind is likely to be cultivated, and they are barely conducive to what the report's authors called "the constructive discharge of the responsibilities of citizenship." But they are perfectly serviceable to elites who do not want an educated, free-thinking citizenry to make "excessive" demands on them.

That is why any movement devoted to abolishing education debt cannot solely be aimed at limited economic reforms. Efforts to lower interest rates, restore bankruptcy protections (currently denied to student debtors), or implement stronger programs for income-based repayment will provide a slice of relief to some, but they will not come close to accomplishing, and may only forestall, the goal of establishing free education as a binding

Cooper Union under student occupation,
May 2013 (courtesy the author)

democratic right. To promote that goal, we will need a movement driven by the principle that equates free education with a free citizenry. Today, as a consequence of the prodigious power of high finance, we face a real "crisis of democracy," not the concoction sold to the Trilateral Commission. The capacity of lenders and investors to treat education as a profit center (student loans are among the most lucrative of all forms of credit) is arguably the most telling symptom of that power. But it would be wrong to conclude that their conduct is merely opportunistic, and that they are exploiting loopholes, opened up by corruptible lawmakers, to maximize their returns. On the contrary, the use of higher education to extract economic rents and foreclose students' futures has been an emerging principle of governance for more than three decades now, with stark consequences for the political disposition of young people.

Passing on the costs of financing education to indebted students typifies the transfer of fiscal responsibility from the state to the private individual that is the chief hallmark of neoliberalism. As almost everyone now knows, the rate of transfer has quickened in recent years, driving up tuition costs in all sectors, but in public universities in particular (tuition costs have risen by 500 percent since 1985, and, in the five years since the crash, are up 27 percent beyond overall inflation). Federal and state governments are fast exiting the business of directly funding higher education. Overall funding by states has fallen by 25 percent since 2000, and some states, such as Arizona and New Hampshire, have cut as much of 50 percent of their spending on education since 2008 alone.[2] As a result, the price gap between leading public institutions and private ones is narrowing sharply by the year. In the public mind, the "privatization of education" is typically characterized by university-industry partnerships, intellectual property grabs, corporate sponsorship and ownership of research, or "contract education"—whereby a firm will pay a community college to upskill its trainees. But the quintessential act of privatization is this shift in responsibility from public provision to private debt-funding on the part of the very people that colleges are supposed to serve. The agenda for accomplishing this transfer is driven by government policy, as are all neoliberal initiatives. Correspondingly, the overall outcome is no longer the equalization of opportunity through education, as it has been exalted by presidential voices, from Eisenhower to Obama. Debt-financing of education has become a reliable contributing factor in the net wealth transfer to the richest Americans from those with the least resources.

In June 2013, the Congressional Budget Office (CBO) forecast that the federal government would realize a profit of $51 billion that year from student loan borrowers. This revelation had a minor seismic impact. For many, it was difficult to digest the concept that a government could actually profit from its obligation to citizens, but the magnitude of the sum stunned even those who knew that the federal loan program had long been a tidy source of revenue. Elizabeth Warren, the newly elected senator from Massachusetts, led the rhetorical charge on Capitol Hill against the Department of Education, pointing out that $51 billion was "more than the annual profit of any Fortune 500 company and about five times the profit of Google." (More to the point, perhaps, it was the equivalent of the combined earnings of the four largest banks in the U.S.—JPMorgan Chase, Bank of America, Citigroup, and Wells Fargo). The author of two reputable scholarly books about bankruptcy, Warren had recently staked her claim as the creditors' new watchdog by introducing legislation, the Bank on Students Loan Fairness Act, that would have slashed the high interest rates (running from 6.8

percent to 7.9 percent) on federal loans to match the rate (0.75 percent) that banks paid to borrow from the Federal Reserve. She and the bill's co-sponsor John Tierney bemoaned the fact that "the federal government makes 36 cents on every dollar it lends to students," and called on Congress to afford student borrowers the same treatment as banks, adding the all-important reminder that "unlike big banks, students do not have armies of lobbyists and lawyers."[3]

Foremost among the creditors applying pressure through their lobbyists was Sallie Mae, the scruple-free queen of student lending, which, at its go-go peak in 2005, had weighed in as the second-most profitable company in the U.S.[4] Accustomed to getting results from leaning on lawmakers, it had already spent more than $1.4 million in the first quarter of 2013 trying to block the progress of two student loan reform bills—the Private Student Loan Bankruptcy Fairness Act and the Fairness for Struggling Students Act—before the one sponsored by Warren and Tierney was dropped in the hopper.[5] Sallie Mae had lately been targeted, at the annual shareholder meeting, by student and union activists, allied with Jobs with Justice, for these mercenary tactics. In a sign of the times, more than 35 percent of its shareholders supported a resolution demanding increased transparency and disclosure from the company's executives.[6]

Warren and Tierney's proposal was as much a sideswipe at the government's deferential treatment of banks as it was a call for fairness in lending. But the fresh scrutiny of federal student lending, inspired by the CBO's forecast, revealed just how much the Department of Education functioned like a Wall Street bank itself. As is common in the finance industry, the lender is allowed to book the projected lifetime earnings of a loan at the time of its origination. Just as a bank will report its future income ($70,000, say, from a loan of $40,000) in the present, thereby inflating its assets, so the government agency builds that estimate into its annual profits. Moreover, the federal government borrows money for virtually nothing (the Treasury bill rate is still rock-bottom), while it lends to students at much higher rates, and reaps the benefits from the spread. Most cruel of all, the profits are not ploughed back into education. They are being used to pay down government debt, much of which should be classified as odious debt since it was contracted to pay the costs of an unlawful war in Iraq and the equally illegitimate bailouts of big banks. In other words, the proceeds from student loans are subsidizing militarism and Wall Street criminality.

Given the fierce appetite on Capitol Hill for reducing the federal debt, there was little chance that the legislative efforts of Warren and Tierney to reduce student loan rates would succeed. Student debtors, who number around forty million, may be defaulting at the rate of a million annually (with one in six in default overall), but the government's collection agencies are able to take advantage of the high penalties, powers of garnishment, and lack of bankruptcy protection to recover as much as 120 percent of each defaulted loan. Having pledged itself to a strict regime of fiscal discipline, the Obama administration had little leeway to take a position that would disrupt or divert the flow of government revenue away from deficit reduction. Any change was likely to be cosmetic, and calculated to register as a PR win—doing what we can to help needy students out. When the dust settled, in July 2013, after a grandstanding debate in Congress, it appeared that the White House had sided with GOP hawks in their drive to reduce the budget deficit by tying federal loan rates to market rates. Undergraduate loan recipients would be paying 3.85 percent—the current yield on the ten-year Treasury note plus 2.05 percent. Rates would be allowed to climb to 8.25 percent for undergraduates, 9.5 percent for graduate students, and a whopping 10.5 percent for parents, and the CBO did indeed forecast a steep rise in the next few years.

Of course, it is deeply unjust that student debtors are held to high interest rates at a time when all other borrowers are enjoying some of the lowest on record. Nor is it fair that they are denied bankruptcy protections or are subject to high default penalties and garnishment of wages, tax returns, Social Security payments, and even disability checks, or that agencies are empowered to pursue them beyond the grave, collecting from surviving co-signer family members. These conditions, stacked in favor of creditors' profit, were legislated largely at the behest of the finance lobby, but they were all retained intact when the government took over direct responsibility for originating federal loans in 2010. The refusal of Congress to reconsider any of these provisions cannot simply be explained as the result of industry pressure or short-term politicking around the federal deficit. It is also a direct expression of governance often labeled in shorthand as neoliberal. As a result, risks and responsibilities for underwriting the costs of education are reassigned to the most vulnerable, wealth is redistributed upwards through the marketplace for credentials, and debt is wielded as a form of social management.

THE OLD DAYS

The GI Bill of Rights (Servicemen's Readjustment Act of 1944) is rightly remembered as the program that launched the Golden Age of U.S. higher education. It provided free college access to more than eight million war veterans and, along with its low-cost mortgage component, a promise of middle class security to their families. For those who like to attach a pecuniary value to every federal program, a 1988 Congressional study found that every dollar spent on educational benefits under the original GI Bill added seven dollars to the national economy in terms of productivity, consumer spending, and tax revenue. But it would be wrong to view the GI Bill purely as an economic stimulus program or even as an act of providence on the part of a welfare-minded state. The program was largely conceived on the back of fears that returning veterans would be swept up in the social agitation that elites predicted from an increasingly emboldened labor movement. Memories of the 1932 militancy of the Bonus Army vets—denied federal assistance after the First World War—

were still fresh. But the mettle of organized labor was even more pressing. "During the forty-four months from Pearl Harbor to V-J Day," Jeremy Brecher noted, "there were 14,471 strikes involving 6,774,000 strikers, more than during any period of comparable length in United States history." But this activity was soon surpassed (and never matched since) when "the first six months of 1946 marked what the U.S. Bureau of Labor Statistics called 'the most concentrated period of labor-management strife in the country's history.'"[7] In part, the GI Bill was a fiscal measure to maintain the economic growth achieved by wartime production, but it was also directed at defusing the growing power of the organized working class, heading off the threat of socialism, and restoring the household primacy of males, as a generation of women decamped from the factories they had staffed to the Cape Cod homes they would now manage with trickle-down proceeds from the spousal "family wage."

The Cold War subsequently saw a massive expansion of government-funded research, and especially through the National Defense Education Act of 1958, which was spurred by the Soviet Union's launch of Sputnik the year before. Under the aegis of competitive militarism, the much-vaunted dominance of the U.S. research university was established through the policy decision to use academia to research and develop science-intensive war technologies.[8] Among other infusions of money, the 1958 bill funded the National Defense Student Loan program, extending low-interest student loans to college students who were focused on scientific and technological education. These were the first direct federal student loans, capitalized with Treasury funds, and they were explicitly aimed at creating a technically skilled workforce as an arm of the warfare, not the welfare, state.

Federal student loans to the general population, along with grants and scholarships for lower-income and minority students, were introduced in the 1965 Higher Education Act (HEA). This bill was one of Lyndon B. Johnson's Great Society programs, crafted in response to civil rights protests and renewed demands of the trade unions for working-class access to college. For the first time, guaranteed student loans were also made available. These were originated by private banks, but backed by the federal government. While the loans were initially limited to low income students—up to $1,000 for households with income less than $15,000—eligibility was gradually expanded under pressure from the banks, and in 1978, the program was opened to all students regardless of income. The formula for healthy profits was now in place. Since the federal guarantees meant risk-free lending for Wall Street, the program functioned as a lavish entitlement for bankers. For the next three decades, the banks, state and federal legislators, and university administrators engaged in a complicated dance over the virtues of guaranteed vs. direct lending. The excesses of the financial industry, combined with the post-crash credit crisis, resolved the debate in 2010, when the Obama administration terminated the Federal Family Education Loan (FFEL) program under which the government had heavily subsidized private banks to provide loans. Today, 85 percent of all loans originate with the federal government, though the faster issuance rate for private loans (which carry higher interest rates) means that this percentage will decrease in the years to come. As of July 2012, private student debt totaled more than $165 billion, with 850,000 loans in default.[9]

HEA had opened doors but its reauthorization, every five years on average, was an opportunity for banks to push their cause. Each iteration sweetened the pot for Wall Street firms who, by the 1980s, were in hot pursuit of new debtors. Federal subsidies and interest rates were progressively hiked, and, in 1972, the Student Loan Marketing Association (aka Sallie Mae) was formed to create a secondary debt market. Like Fannie Mae before it, this new government-sponsored enterprise initially bought loans from banks in order to free up their books for more lending. States were also authorized under the Tax Reform Act of 1976 to create another secondary market through non-profit corporations, set up to buy the loans. Enjoying the benefits of these markets, the 100 percent federal loan guarantees, and a raft of other subsidies from the government, private lenders raked in profits. Cumulative student debt, which stood at $1.8 billion in 1977, began to rise more rapidly, reaching $30 billion in 1996.[10]

By the time the Cold War wound down in the early 1990s, the taxpayer revolts had already taken a heavy toll on state budgets, slicing deeply into support for public colleges. California's Proposition 13 cap on property taxes turned into a fiscal instrument for realizing ex-governor Ronald Reagan's personal vendetta against the University of California system. In his election bid, Reagan had profiled the student protester as a public enemy. He lambasted participants in Berkeley's Free Speech Movement as "freaks," "brats," and "cowardly fascists," declared that "education is a privilege, not a right," and argued that "the state should not subsidize intellectual curiosity." Though he zealously mobilized the National Guard against Berkeley's protesters, cut education budgets, and hiked fees in an effort to hasten tuition-based funding, the system was still protected by its alumni elites.[11] But the revenue shortfall from Prop 13's impact produced a more technocratic opportunity, wrung dry of Reagan's ideological hostility, for ratcheting down state support and passing on costs to students.

Public universities like California's continued to be vital Cold War assets, indispensable as research arms for the military-industrial complex. But with the end of the Cold War, the need for Washington to compete with the socialist bloc in high-profile sectors of public provision dissolved. Higher education was one of them. Funding for big science was cut, and the federal pipeline flow to universities dropped off. Private capital was brought on to campuses to help plug the gaps as administrators turned toward university-industry partnerships for new sources of research funding. In the meantime, the tax revolts spread nationwide, with a predictable impact on states' direct funding of colleges. From the mid-1990s, college costs began to rise sharply, and students from higher-income households were increasingly forced to take out loans. The entry of these lower-risk borrowers prompted the major banks to jump into the ever more lucrative sector, now juiced up by the advent of securitization in the form of Student Loan Asset Backed Securities (SLABS), first issued by Sallie Mae in 1995.

Spun off that same year, and completely privatized by 2004, Sallie Mae reinforced its growing dominance in the industry by acquiring a host of lenders, collection agencies, guarantee agencies, and consolidators, many of them non-profit. No other lender was in a position to control every aspect of the debt process—from loan origination to servicing and collection. Lack of oversight combined with its near-monopoly of the sector generated fraud in every corner of the student loan landscape. Kickbacks for financial aid counselors, predatory "subprime" targeting of low-income students, and abusive harassment from collectors were just some of the routine malpractices of Sallie Mae, followed by the other banks that thrived on the lack of legal protections for student debtors. While the 2010 reorganization of federal loans cut the banks off from direct lending, Sallie Mae was one of four companies selected to administer and service the loans, ensuring a continued, healthy profit from the allocation of government funds. The firm's dominance of private lending has only increased, now that some of the too-big-to-fail banks, dismayed by the rising tide of defaults, have exited the business. Though Congress ended its federal charter in 2004, Sallie Mae is not only the largest originator of (pre-2010) federal loans; it continues to trade on the public perception that its private lending operations are backed by the government. This is not happenstance. The federal government's administration of higher education has long been a conduit for private profit—whether for defense contractors during the Cold War, or Wall Street banks during the heyday of student debt-financing.

The crudest, and most debased, form of that relationship can be found in the for-profit college sector, increasingly the default option for low-income or "non-traditional" students shut out of the strapped public college systems. Profits in this sector, which now accounts for a quarter of all higher education institutions in the U.S., depend primarily on indirect revenue from federal loans. For-profits now accommodate between 10 and 13 percent of enrolled students, but they receive 25 percent of all federal loan dollars. Increasingly acquired by publicly-traded companies and private equity firms, they have become Wall Street's colleges, devoting an ever larger portion of revenue to marketing, recruitment, and shareholder profit, and a dwindling share to instruction. A 2010 investigation by the Senate Health, Education, Labor, and Pensions Committee found that for-profits charge four times the cost of degree programs at comparable community colleges; 96 percent of their students take out federal loans (compared to 13 percent at community colleges), while as many as 63 percent leave without a degree; and more than one in five students default within three years of entering repayment, accounting for almost 47 percent of federal loan defaulters.[12]

The statistics of excessive debt, default, and daylight robbery in this sector are staggering. Yet the for-profit boom is primarily a result of the state withdrawal from public education that has left many households in the cold. In some states, especially in the Deep South, community colleges have opted out of the federal loan program, disproportionately affecting African American populations.[13] Would-be students have no choice but to turn to private lenders who target high-risk borrowers, or else they have to take the federal loans on offer to attend a more dodgy for-profit college. While visiting a community college in the Southwest, I was told by a son of immigrants that he had taken out a series of loans, on the advice of "admissions counselors," to enroll at a for-profit college, only to discover upon graduation that the institution was not properly accredited. Unable to transfer credit, he was starting afresh at a new institution, with a new round of loans. Even families with generations of college experience have difficulty sifting through the many financial aid options available today. For first generation families like his, access to accurate information is not readily available, and they are more easily duped by false advertising targeted directly at them. Indeed, the Consumer Financial Protection Bureau (CFPB) found that 12 percent of students who take out private student debt don't ever apply for federal loans, carrying lower interest rates and more flexible repayment terms, even though they would have qualified to receive them.[14]

Private college graduates from middle-income families are the poster children for student debt. Mainstream media producers feast on the stories of these "profligate" individuals who have racked up $200,000 or more of debt. But the real story lies lower down the income scale. As with every other form of personal debt, the overall impact of student debt is magnified among low-income families. Not surprisingly, a familiar racial profile emerges. Of those who have earned bachelor's degrees, about 81 percent of African American students and 67 percent of Latin@ students leave school with debt, as compared to 64 percent of white students.[15] Hit hard by the wipeout of equity from the subprime mortgage bust, black families have had to borrow more for college, and so the rate of default for African-American student debtors is four times that of whites. But even in 2007-2008, just before the crash, 27 percent of Black graduates were borrowing more than $30,000 to pay for college, compared with 16 percent of whites, 14 percent of Latin@s, and 9 percent of Asian Americans.[16] An unequal debt burden is also carried by LGBTQ students. Their families are often unsupportive, making it difficult to find co-signers for federal PLUS loans available to parents to help pay for their child's tuition. Under these circumstances, they are at the mercy of high-rate lenders. In the same boat are undocumented students—the Dream Generation—who are legally excluded from federal loans and are generally ineligible for state or university-funded financial aid.

Native Americans, African Americans and Latin@s were largely excluded from the home ownership and education benefits of the original GI Bill. There were high hopes that this historic neglect would be remedied by the new GI Bill (Post-9/11 Veterans Education Assistance Act) introduced by Congress in 2008 to help veterans of the wars in Iraq and Afghanistan enter the higher education system. Yet the issuance of the funds, to the tune of $9 billion annually, proved to be an invitation for recruiters from the for-profit colleges to aggressively pursue ex-soldiers—some vets with traumatic brain injuries had no memory of signing up for classes but were pressed for payment. The result was an undue impact on veterans of color, who had served disproportionately in the armed services.[17] These proprietary colleges had exploited a legislative loophole that allows them to count GI Bill monies (issued from the Defense Department) as part of the 10 percent of revenue they are required to raise from sources other than the Department of Education. Federal student loans from that source account for the other 90 percent of their revenue. As a result of their targeting of "dollars in uniforms," more than 38 percent of the GI Bill government funds found their way into the coffers of Wall Street's colleges.[18]

The report issued by Tom Harkin's 2010 Senate committee was not the first scathing Congressional indictment of for-profit college education. Sam Nunn conducted investigations in the mid-1970s, and then again, in 1994, in a series of high-profile hearings. Hair-raising testimony about industry abuses persuaded Congress to set regulatory rules that were weakened over the years by hardcore lobbying. But this was nothing compared with the pushback against the Obama administration's efforts to follow through on the 2010 report. The $30 billion industry dispatched a battalion of lobbyists to Capitol Hill, many of them former Democratic Party insiders with close ties to the White House, as part of a formidable campaign to sabotage the proposed stiffening of regulatory rules. A portion of the $16 million war chest went to Richard Gephardt, regarded as a "liberal lion" in his heyday as House majority leader. Like so many other former lawmakers, he now has a lucrative career fronting for corporations he had once been elected to regulate. The lobbying blitzkrieg, which was considered extreme even by K Street standards, succeeded in watering down the proposed rules.[19]

Notwithstanding such well-intentioned but ultimately thwarted efforts, the longstanding inability of lawmakers to check the mercurial growth of predatory Wall Street colleges is not an example of failed policymaking. On the contrary, the emergence of the sector, in parallel with the general growth of student debt, can be seen as a direct result of neoliberal governance through the administration of education. In the Cold War era of managed capitalism, state funding of higher education was part of a compact to deliver middle-class income and consumer comforts to working people and their children, but it also underwrote the Pentagon's tight relationship with defense contractors and other corporations with vested interests in a permanent war economy. When finance began to outpace industrial manufacturing as the dominant profit stream in American capitalism, higher education proved to be just as serviceable. The spigot of debt service to Wall Street was opened wide when the right to access loans was extended to all, in the name of fairness in lending. Just as the research university was scaled up to meet Cold War needs, so the mushrooming for-profit sector sprang up as the fastest delivery track for debt rents, while its packaging of educational services fully reflects the neoliberal ideal of a pay-per society.

ASSET BUBBLE OR POLITICAL MOVEMENT?

Unlike other kinds of household debt, which began to fall off after the recession set in, student debt has continued its rise, climbing among all age groups, along with college costs. Clearly, the student loan burden is not part of the "debt overhang" from the crash. In fact, its rate of accumulation has accelerated since 2008, as state after state sliced their education budgets. A much-noted Federal Reserve report, in March 2013, recorded that student debt almost tripled between 2004 and 2012, and that student loan delinquencies (balances past due for 90 days or more) were rising precipitously. Nearly one-third of borrowers in repayment were in default.[20]

The default rates stoked fresh fears that student debt was the next asset bubble to burst. These concerns were further reinforced by news that the SLABS market had regained its appeal to investors. SLABS trading had grown from $75.6 million in 1990 to $2.67 trillion at its peak just before the crash, though market volume has fallen off since then.[21] In March 2013, when

Sallie Mae sold $1.1 billion of SLABS securities backed by private student loans, investors' demand for the highest-risk tranche turned out to be fifteen times greater than the supply.[22] Yet this resurgence of the appetite for purchasing risky loans probably had more to do with the desperation of investors in an era of low interest rates. Even though Sallie Mae issued a sizable $13.8 billion worth of SLABS in 2012, this volume was a drop in the bucket compared to the pre-2008 trade in unsecured subprime securities.[23] If mortgage securities turn bad, there is always a house somewhere that can be repossessed, but SLABS, which are mostly government-backed, have no underlying physical asset that can be foreclosed and seized, or traded to others. Education is an inalienable asset—at least until banks can develop software to download it from debtors' brains!

If there is a student debt bubble, it is less a financial liability than a social catastrophe. The nation's economic managers fret about stalled growth because heavily indebted graduates may never be able to afford a home, or children, let alone the other big-ticket consumer items that move the GDP upwards. Some reform groups have proposed mass debt forgiveness as a utilitarian way to "stimulate the economy."[24] More radical voices reject the paradigm of forgiveness (with its connotations of culpability), and call for a student debt jubilee, on moral grounds, to relieve the human suffering that accompanies this modern form of debt bondage. In any case, the suffering is no longer hidden, because debtors have broken the customary silence around debt by speaking out publicly about their painful circumstances.

Among the more conspicuous protesters at Occupy locations around the country were underemployed graduates sporting debt-confession signs—"I Owe $120,000," or "I Can't (Won't) Pay My Student Debts"—and many were vocal about their desperation, both in the face-to-face agora and in online compilations of testimony, like the popular "We Are the 99 Percent" Tumblr.[25] This public ritual of "coming out" about debt felt like the stirring of a political movement. At the very least, it was a way of exorcizing the shame that privately afflicts debtors and that can put them on the pathway to depression, divorce, and suicide. [26]

At New York University (NYU), where I teach, students graduate with 40 percent more debt than the national average. By some estimates, it is the single most expensive American university (for the 2013-14 academic year, tuition, room and board, and required fees added up to $61,977), and you don't have to look hard to find graduates who owe jaw-dropping sums of money.[27] One alumnus wrote to tell me that he and his peers had formed a "hundred club" for those in the six-figure debt bracket. A staple of student lore is the widely reported information that NYU has the highest-number of college "Sugar Babies" on a "dating" website that matches young women with older, male "Sugar Daddies." With limited financial aid, students at the largest private university in the U.S. are among the most compromised in their desperate search for ways to stay afloat.

I had known for some time that my paycheck depends on my students going deeply into debt, often for decades to come. But like most of my colleagues, I chose not to dwell on it, a decision that seemed justifiable given that faculty salaries have been stagnant for so long. Indeed, instructional costs, which have been sliced as a result of the casualization of the academic workforce, have almost nothing to do with the breakneck growth of college tuition costs. By contrast, administrative "bloat" ranks high on the list of contributing factors.[28] According to the U.S. Department of Education, the number of university employees hired to manage or administer people, programs, and regulations increased 50 percent faster than the number of instructors between 2001 and 2011, and their salaries have also risen at a much faster rate than those of faculty.[29] Administrators and their staff now outnumber fulltime faculty in American universities. Unlike in corporate America, where layers of management were cut away in pursuit of the "lean and mean" enterprise, colleges have been fattening the managerial payroll. Other non-classroom costs have ballooned, foremost among them the bills for capital-intensive building expansion. The cost of borrowing for construction is a jumbo component of the debt load carried by many colleges, and student tuition, as Bob Meister has shown, is not only the collateral for securing the construction bonds but also the funding source for paying the interest on them.[30] Indeed, total institutional debt at public four-year colleges more than tripled between 2002 and 2011, to $88 billion, according to the Department of Education.[31]

Urban universities, in particular, are ever more central to a city's growth machine, and so there are many incentives to expand their physical footprint even at the cost of being financially overleveraged.[32] The NYU administration has pursued its own, controversial plan to expand—the largest development proposal in downtown Manhattan for several decades—with an estimated initial price tag of $5 billion. Raising this sum would require debt-financing far in excess of the current university endowment—at $2.1 billion—and the long-term debt load, at $3.7 billion (up from $998 million in 2003). Even Moody's, a reliable champion of university expansion, characterized NYU's balance sheet as "highly leveraged," citing the university's 0.51 ratio of "expendable financial resources to direct debt" as "thin." The acceptable ratio for non-profits in general is from 0.8 to 2.0, but most universities try to stay well above 1.0. Fierce faculty resistance to the expansion plan was based, in part, on the near-certainty that financing would require hefty increases in tuition and overall student debt.[33] Indeed, universities are generally able to secure good credit ratings (enabling them to borrow more cheaply) because they can raise tuition fees at will. Unlike most other businesses, they have a built-in capacity to increase revenue year in year out.

Although student debt lay at the core of NYU's fiscal being, whenever I brought it up as a topic of class discussion, I found that no one was in a great hurry to volunteer their thoughts. This was not at all the norm for a cohort who freely offer up their personal opinions and sentiments on most subjects. When I quizzed them privately, two students explained that the volume of their loans was a source of profound shame. At a pricey college, they were surrounded by full-freight peers from well-heeled families, and so they feared the stigma if they spoke about their own straitened circumstances. One of them apologized for falling asleep in class: he had taken on a second job—not uncommon these days—to avoid the burden of even more loans. The other confessed that she did not want to feed any inner doubts about whether her dream education would be a career stepping stone or a financial millstone. As long as she was still studying, she wanted to stave off such thoughts.

Visits to other campuses confirmed my experience at NYU. Students I met generally did not think of their loans as debt at all; they had no reason to imagine what it would feel like to make monthly payments. One referred to his loans as "funny money," another described them as a "hedge" (using the language of finance) or a bet against his future. Few considered themselves to be debtors. In fact, ethnographic evidence shows that those with outstanding loans don't think of themselves as "debtors" until they actually fall behind in their payments.[34] People with mortgage loans, like me, think of ourselves as homeowners, not housing debtors, though the latter label is more accurate. Automatic debiting from our bank accounts has removed the monthly ritual of writing a debt-service check that might have once allowed for self-examination, doubt, or defiance.

Most student borrowers take it on trust when they are presented with a loan package, and few have any financial literacy to speak of. The loan offer does not invite reflection because it has become a normalized feature of college life. No doubt, this smooth routinization helps to ease the guilt of the admissions officers who are paid to reassure recruits that high-interest loans are a solid investment in their futures. Those with less conscience have been caught colluding directly with lenders.[35] Parents, for their part, don't ask too many questions. They are cowed by the prestige of colleges, or are anxious not to puncture their children's aspirations. Yet students and their families surely have a right to know how administrators are spending the ever-larger tuition checks. While the books of private colleges remain closed, and the fiscal affairs of many public universities are murky, to say the least, there is a growing movement to demand fiscal transparency.

At my institution, the clamor notched up after revelations that the administration had an undisclosed program for extending forgivable loans to senior officers and star faculty for housing purchases. Most notoriously, the program had enabled the purchase of vacation homes, including a million dollar beach house for the president himself.[36] The stark contrast between the treatment of student loans and the forgivable ones at the top typified a double standard that has become ever more apparent with the rising levels of compensation of college presidents and their favored administrators. Since debt-financed education has serviced their own bank accounts so lavishly, it is no surprise that the voices of university presidents have been conspicuously absent from public debate about the student debt crisis. They seem content to weather the current storm.

Nor is it likely that college costs will stabilize until demand falls off, and even if this were to happen nationally, the growth in overseas demand—fueled by the desire of the swelling middle class in rapidly developing countries for brand-name degrees—will probably help to make up the deficit. According to a British Council report, global tertiary education enrollments reached 170 million in 2009, up 160 percent since 1990, and were expected to continue multiplying, though at a slightly reduced pace, over the next decade.[37] Such rosy estimates may well dictate how college administrators, faced with further cuts from their state legislatures, react to fiscal quandaries. Dependence on tuition payments from international students is already high—foreign students make up the majority of enrollments in U.S. graduate programs in many STEM (science, technology, engineering, and mathematics) fields—and the rush to establish offshore programs and branch campuses is being driven by the same pursuit of debt-free revenue. There are many risks involved in such ventures, especially those located in authoritarian countries.[38] But the prospect of adding overseas revenue streams will continue to attract higher education's fiscal managers, driven by desperation, or ambition, or simply by their training in neoliberal economics.

YOU ARE NOT A LOAN

In November 2011, I helped to launch the Occupy Student Debt Campaign (www.occupystudentdebtcampaign.org), which invited debtors to pledge to refuse payments after one million others had signed up. Millions were defaulting in private, and our pledge was designed (hastily, in order to utilize the viral energy of Occupy) to offer a more self-empowering way of taking action and focusing public attention on the issue. Attracting pledges was not easy, although several thousand did sign on. We had few resources to run a national campaign, and our efforts were sabotaged by the lending industry, whose representatives are quick to target any form of opposition, and by reformers, wholly focussed on lobbying Congress. Nonetheless, we helped to raise national awareness of the student debt crisis, and we publicly introduced the concept of student debt refusal, before retiring the campaign. The time, we concluded, was not yet ripe for a full-blown debt refusal movement, and the vehicle we had chosen was one that needed more campaign support than was available. Ironically, one million debtors did privately default over the course of the next year. If they had collectively defaulted as a form of economic disobedience, the political impact would have been profound.

The campaign rested on four principles that received a good public airing, and are still viable: 1) Public education should be free—at that time, we estimated the annual cost, to the federal government, of covering the tuition of all students enrolled in two and four year public colleges would be a mere $70 billion; 2) Loans should be interest-free—no one, least of all the government, should profit from education; 3) Universities and colleges should open up their books in the interest of full fiscal transparency—students and their

Occupy Student Debt Campaign, street march on 1T Day, April 25, 2012 (courtesy Giles Clark)

families have a right to know; 4) Existing debt should be written off, jubilee-style, as a single, corrective act. Each of these principles differed in kind from the reformist talk about student loan forgiveness, a moralistic term that implied debtors had done something wrong. Promoting the right to free education was to dwell in a different moral universe from the bare-knuckle Capitol Hill brawls over whether to raise or lower federal loan interest rates by a point or two.

By the end of the summer, President Obama announced a reform plan, aimed at reorienting the government's approach to higher education funding. The platform was cobbled together from the performance-based criteria favored by his Education Secretary, Arne Duncan, and others who advocate for turning education into a competitive arena where colleges fight over reward-driven rankings. In Obama's scheme, universities would be induced to rein in costs by providing more "value" to students and taxpayers. Metrics, based on how many students graduate and how much they earn, would be used to stagger student loan rates and Pell Grant awards. Also encouraged as part of the pursuit of this "value" were the kind of initiatives that are opposed by the vast majority of academic professionals, such as increased vocational learning and MOOCs —"massive online open courses" made widely available to participants through interactive web-based networks.

Notwithstanding that colleges have little to zero influence over the employment climate, let alone compensation levels, the Obama approach is underpinned by a conviction that the chief purpose of higher education is to deliver workplace-ready recruits in the most cost-effective way.[39] The complex and expensive bureaucratic method for overseeing this vision stands in stark contrast to the simple moral case for the U.S. to join the long list of countries (all of them less affluent) around the world that offer tuition-free higher education as a citizenly right. In the twentieth century, the nation's managers made the decision to fully fund K-12 education because they wanted a stable middle class and a showcase democracy. Extending the coverage to tertiary education in the twenty-first century is essential to rebuilding a functional middle class, capable, at the very least, of fulfilling its customary role, for these economic managers, as a consumer of last resort within the global marketplace. They would rather not have an educated, free-thinking citizenry on their hands, but creditor elites do need a population with enough disposable income to pay debt service and to buy big-ticket items, though preferably with the help of loans.

On even more pragmatic grounds, a huge chunk of the current tuition bill could be secured, according to Robert Samuels, Mike Konczal, and others, simply by eliminating all of the tax credits and exemptions that currently subsidize the student loan system.[40] Everyone knows that college costs are too high, but hardly anyone is aware of how little it would cost to make college in the U.S. free. According to Strike Debt's updated estimate, students in the 2010-2011 school year spent $59.9 billion on tuition for public colleges and universities. Subtracting all of the existing credits (such as the American Opportunity and HOPE tax credits) and exemptions (for loan interest) would save $37.15 billion. Reclaiming public money (Pell Grants and GI Bill funds) that is inappropriately allocated to for-profit colleges amounts to $10.35 billion. All these savings add up to $47.25 billion, leaving just $12.4 billion to be accounted for.[41] That is all it would cost in additional funding to make public higher education entirely free. A paltry sum when put alongside the tens of billions unaccounted for in the defense spending system, or the equally large sums of taxpayer money used to subsidize banks and corporations. Additional levies could be extracted by withdrawing the tax-free status enjoyed by private colleges, heavily dependent, as they are, on federal loan revenue and other government grants.

From an international perspective, the political economy of U.S. education is an outlier, but its debt-financing model, along with its proprietary colleges, are being exported abroad. In England, government cuts recently forced universities to introduce massive fee hikes, though they remain free in Scotland, where I was educated in the 1970s, and where there remains vigorous support among the populace for maintaining adequate levels of state provision for education as a social right. Student resistance to U.S.-style privatization has also been strong, most prominently in the mass protest movements in Chile and Quebec in 2011-12. The red square insignia of the Quebec movement (*carrément dans le rouge*) has been adopted internationally as a symbol of debt resistance. When the Occupy Student Debt Campaign joined with other Occupy groups to form the Strike Debt alliance in the early summer of 2013, the meaning of the red square was further adapted—the four corners symbolized education, medical, housing, and credit card. Practically speaking, these four kinds of debt are likely to be circulating, in an interdependent fashion, through any given household unit. Focusing on the individual profiles of student debts and debtors tends to overlook how connected these kinds of loans are, and so the formation of Strike Debt was an effort to better illustrate how debt binds us all.

On one of my campus visits, for example, a student told me that her father had been laid off, and so the family had fallen behind in its mortgage payments. Her father was a co-signer for her loans, for which the family home was collateral, but he had also been using separate home equity loans to pay some of her college bills. That source of credit was now closed off, and the family's balance sheets were deep in negative territory. At the same time, her parents were landed with some of her grandmother's hospital bills. To bring some relief to a household that had been hit by what she called "a perfect storm of debt," she had considered dropping out. Instead, she had turned to her two credit cards as an alternate source for funding her degree, opening up yet another door for creditors to come knocking, and joining the one-third of the U.S student body that pays tuition with their credit cards.[42] Fading fast were the college dreams of her younger sister. Newly graduated from high school, she was about to join her mother on payroll at their local Walmart Supercenter to help tide over the family.

Public burning of Sallie Mae student debt statement, with Reverend Billy officiating, 1T Day, April 25, 2012 (courtesy Sarah McDaniel)

Before it achieved higher visibility through the *Debt Resistors' Operations Manual* and the Rolling Jubilee (described in the last chapter), Strike Debt built its base around the movement's coming-out ritual by holding a series of "debtors' assemblies" every Sunday in New York City parks. Largely unstructured, these were open invitations to speak out publicly. The crowds were small enough for some intimacy, and the atmosphere, while informal, was often electrifying. It was heart-rending to hear speakers bear witness about how debt had blocked their aspirations and forced them into decisions they deeply regretted. Many spoke of long bouts of depression, some of divorce and personal loss, while others described the kind of future—owning a home, having children—they believed was now hopelessly unattainable. Parents stood up to agonize about their responsibility, as co-signers, for the loans of their now unemployed offspring. A fellow activist reminded us of an even more harrowing predicament: She had contracted a life-threatening ailment, and the bitter prospect of dying young was sharpened by the knowledge that her low-income parents would inherit her debts.

NOT MARRIED TO THE MOOC

In the absence of an organized student debt movement, policymakers will take their cues from the solutions offered by business and administrative elites. A currently favored one comes in the form of the technical fix known as MOOCs. The tidal wave of hype attending their rollout in 2011-2012 was unusual, even by Silicon Valley's standards for next-generation technologies. Even so, the MOOC concept is not all that innovative. After all, online education has been the mainstay of for-profit colleges like the University of Phoenix for more than a decade, and MIT's OpenCourseWare launched as early as 2002. Nor is the open access broadcasting model a breakthrough. Radio was widely envisaged as a medium of instruction in the 1920s, and Britain's Open University has been conducting multimedia teaching and issuing degrees to millions from the early 1970s. But the pioneer MOOC providers (two Silicon Valley startups, Udacity and Coursera, and the non-profit EdX) launched at exactly the time that policymakers were looking for a magic bullet to make higher education more accessible and affordable. It was telling that the proposed cure came in the form of encouragement for venture capitalists to treat colleges as a fresh source of profit. In the case of non-profit EdX, the solution was an elite formula ("Ivy League for the masses") for communicating the "sage on the stage" wisdom of star professors at exclusive universities like Harvard, MIT, Berkeley, McGill, and Georgetown to audiences of lesser mortals. For many of their critics, MOOCs represented a new front in the race to privatize higher education. Others saw the EdX transmission model as a recipe for further devaluing credentials, since a MOOC degree would presumably carry even less weight in the world of employment.

Some economists were quick to see the MOOC as a solution to the "cost disease" diagnosed by William Baumol in the 1960s. According to this theory, originally advanced in a study of the performing arts, costs are condemned to rise in labor-intensive industries like health care and education because they cannot take advantage of productivity increases through automation or technological innovation.[43] The problem with using this theory to explain skyrocketing tuition is that there is no evidence of appreciable growth in instructional costs. As Rudy Fichtenbaum and Hank Reichman point out, public college salaries have actually been stagnant or in decline for some time: "the average salary for a full-time faculty member at a public institution in 1999-2000 was $77,897. In 2011-12, the same figure in constant dollars was $77,843."[44] Factor in the overall cost savings from the rapid casualization of college teaching—a vast majority of instructors are contingent employees now—and the decline is even more pronounced. By contrast, the corresponding rise in administrators' salaries would be a more relevant factor, but the costs of bureaucracy are not central to the Baumol Effect.

Only in a skewed neoliberal universe, where everything is valued for its capacity to produce revenue, would education and healthcare, not to mention the arts, be obliged to show relative market efficiencies. Yet even in countries which regard these sectors as essential social services and not as "industries," the cost of provision by the state is much lower than the price outcomes of the market mechanisms increasingly favored in the U.S. Reflecting on the cost disease model in a more recent book, Baumol notes that a society that benefits from increasing wealth could choose to subsidize the relative costs in an "inefficient" sector like education and healthcare.[45] After all, this is what many other countries do, through general taxation, in the conviction that public education and public health generate indispensable benefits to society at large.

In the U.S. system, however, the burden of proof of education's value falls on each individual's cost-benefit analysis—i.e. the balance between upfront costs in student loans and lifetime benefits in income returns. In response to mounting concerns about the student debt burden, more and more data has to be presented to support the belief that "investing" in a college education produces real economic value. The returns to college attendance are often computed to be higher than other investments, such as stocks, bonds, and real estate.[46] Over the span of a lifetime, the worth of a generic undergraduate degree has been estimated at anything from $650,000 to $2.7 million.[47] Defenders of the current loan system seldom fail to point out the projected value of this investment, reinforcing the mercenary equation between education and financial return. Yet a recent Demos report estimated that a student who graduates with a bachelor's degree from a four-year university with $53,000 in debts faces a lifetime wealth loss of nearly $208,000.[48] By that same reckoning, the $1.2 trillion in outstanding student loan debt will lead to total lifetime wealth loss of $4.5 trillion for indebted households, with most of the losses resulting from lower retirement savings. For households with larger-than-average levels of student debt—students from low-income families, students of color, and for-profit college students—the losses are much higher. Every loss, moreover, is someone's gain, and so it is just as accurate to represent these figures as profits for the creditor class.

Whether or not they swallow the crude conception of self-worth that regards education solely as an income-generator, most students have generally aspired to end up in the top quintile of earners.[49] But with the top 1 percent increasingly siphoning off the lion's share of wealth, even this promise of a good return has weakened.[50] Chronic underemployment for college graduates in the worst labor market since the Great Depression, combined with the absence of any prospect of debt relief, has fueled talk of a "lost generation." The more proactive debtors are contemplating, or are already pursuing, a life "off the grid," beyond the surveillance orbit of the credit bureaus, and the grasping reach of the banks and debt collectors. Stunned by the double standard displayed by the government's lavish debt relief for Wall Street, many others are awaiting a debtors' movement with the common strength and guts to reclaim the future from the grip of the creditocracy.

When all of life is declared to be open for business, and social goods are viewed as eligible profit centers, why should a particular sector like education be considered off-limits? Michael Sandel has argued that there are sacred areas of social and cultural activity where the profane, amoral logic of markets does not belong. Among those he cites are schools, hospitals, prisons, armies, law enforcement, the legislature, motherhood, and the biosphere. "Markets," he observes, "leave their mark" by altering the goods they trade in.[51] They should be kept in their place, he argues, because the mentality of self-interest that they install lingers even after they have been chased out of the proverbial temple of sacred goods.

Because the tendency to commodify everything in sight is an inexorable part of capitalist logic, efforts, like Sandel's, to separate God from Mammon in the sphere of education have long been a losing battle.[52] But marketization of social goods is one thing, while extracting rents from a lifetime of debt is quite another matter. In the case of student debt, access to the good of education is not being sold as a market commodity, at least not in the way that a house or an automobile is purchased or traded. After all, education, like health, is an inalienable good, with no resale value. Profiting from student debt is therefore a way of preying upon all the personal and public benefits that an individual education might generate. In the case of the commonweal, those benefits can long outlast that person's lifetime. Think of the enduring legacies of great works in the field of culture, science, philosophy, and scholarship in general. An educational debt load can exact a lifetime of economic constraints on individuals. But the more debilitating shackles are those placed on our mental life, where, like William Blake's "mind-forg'd manacles," they will curb the impulse to free inquiry—the wellspring of any liberal society—and stifle any gains to society as a result.

This is why student debts should be regarded as profoundly anti-social. They are hostile to the common good and inimical to human development. Just as sharply as other forms of household debt, they reinforce and magnify patterns of social inequality. The 1965 Higher Education Act, which initiated federal student loans, was framed as a remedy for low-income and minority populations whose access to educational opportunity had been blocked. Yet it also ushered in a system of debt-financing that ended up encumbering those with the least resources. At this point, the choices are increasingly stark. We can carry on watching legislators clash swords over percentage rates on Capitol Hill. Or we can judge this spectator sport to be sadistic, and directly challenge the cruel transaction that it perpetuates. Student debt refusal almost certainly would be an act of civil disobedience, but it might also be the first step in redeeming the future of education, and the productive life that flows from it.

WAGES OF THE FUTURE

In the course of industrialization, the conflict over wages tends to occupy center stage. It still does in manufacturing zones in many developing countries, and it is hardly a thing of the past in economies considered to be post-industrial in their development. But in societies that are heavily financialized, the struggle over debt is increasingly the frontline conflict. Not because wage conflict is over (it never will be), but because debts, for most people, are the wages of the future, to which creditors lay claim far in advance. Each new surrender of a part of our lives to debt-financing further consumes the fruit of labor we have not yet performed in the form of compensation we have not yet earned. Now that this condition has become inescapable, it is easier to imagine that the struggle between creditor and debtor is much older than the face-off between capital and labor that Marx proposed as a common sense explanation for economic life. After all, exploitation through debt long predates the era of wage tyranny, and its recent restoration as the most efficient means of wealth accumulation suggests that credit is a more enduring, all-weather organ of economic power.

Tempting as that conclusion may be, it would be more instructive to dwell on the intimate relationship between labor and debt. Everywhere we look, the history of work is haunted by the specter of insolvency in one form or another. The systematic use of debt to deepen every form of labor exploitation has been constant: from the debt slaves of antiquity, forced by creditors to bond their labor through servitude, to the debt-driven circuits of the African slave trade. A highly selective list would also include the agrarian debt peons and the sharecroppers of the Americas, unable to pay off loans advanced on their harvests, or the yeoman farmers of the Populist era, dependent on lines of credit from Wall Street banks and liable to dispossession under the crop lien system; the factory and railroad workers subsisting on company scrip, or the urban proletariat, at the mercy of pawners and loan sharks; today's transnational migrants, toiling to work off their transit and recruitment debts; and in the low-wage economy, the ubiquitous victims of wage theft, who are effectively financing their employers.[1]

In light of that long historical record, it would not be unreasonable to conclude that very little has changed. Debt bondage or bonded labor is a condition that still affects tens of millions today worldwide. With the rise of financialization, it flourishes in a more indirect form among many more. In his 2004 annual report to Berkshire Hathaway's shareholders, CEO Warren Buffet warned that, contrary to George Bush's vaunted ideal of an "ownership society," the U.S. was becoming more of a "sharecropper's society."[2] Buffet was directly referencing the ballooning trade deficit, and the growing "ownership" of American assets by foreign creditors, though his phrase was more widely taken as a comment on the impact of general indebtedness on the population at large. He had also earned a reputation as one of the few plutocrats to openly acknowledge that the 1 percent has been waging class warfare for some time. "It's my class, the rich class," he observed, "that's making war, and we're winning," which is why he believes they should be paying more of their share of wealth in taxes.[3] Yet Buffet, who enjoys his prominence as someone who "speaks truth *from* power," is simply reprising the advice of Don Fabrizio, the Sicilian aristocrat in Giuseppe di Lampedusa's *The Leopard*, who laconically advised his fellow noblemen: "If we want things to stay as they are, things will have to change." Recognizing that reforms are needed for the creditocracy to survive intact, Buffet's concession takes the form of a devil's deal: we will pay more taxes but only as long as you don't tamper with the system by which we lay our hands on the wealth in the first place. Charles Munger, Buffet's own vice-chairman at Berkshire Hathaway, expressed a view more typical of the creditor class when he told a student audience in 2010 that they should "thank God" for the bailout of Wall Street, while advising them that ordinary Americans in economic distress should just "suck it in and cope." After all, he continued, invoking the social Darwinism that is the gut philosophy of his peers, "if you just start bailing out all the individuals instead of telling them to adapt, the culture dies."[4]

Few would dispute Buffet's admission that financialization has served his class very handily, though there is more resistance to seeing ourselves as the debt peons of his "sharecropper's society." One case in point is the ambivalent response to the use of the term "indenture" to describe student debt.[5] In a knowledge economy, where a college degree is considered a requisite passport to any kind of decent livelihood, most workforce entrants

Protest shield deployed during attempted occupation at Duarte Square, NYC, December 17, 2011 (courtesy Not an Alternative)

must go into debt in return for the right to labor. This kind of contract, it has been argued, is the essence of indenture. Some have gone even further, describing student debt as a neo-feudal condition, where debtors find themselves bound to creditors but are also free to choose their own means of repaying: "a perfect synthesis of modern and ancient systems: all the control of medieval serfdom combined with wage slavery's freedom from any responsibility for individual workers' welfare."[6] While such analogies have been a useful provocation to debtors, stiffening their resentment at their plight, they have also proved offensive to others, on the grounds that the college-educated are too privileged to be compared to bonded laborers. A similar retort is often thrown back at high-wage employees in the technology sector, whose long working hours often give rise to their complaints that they are working in "high-tech sweatshops."

For impoverished people who are formally indentured—including today's migrant or guest workers crisscrossing the globe—labor is owed to whom they are bound. Under such circumstances, employment for the purposes of paying off the bonds is readily available from employers in the chain of credit. The more informal the contract, the more the worker is exploited, and so the fees that migrants pay up front to transit and recruitment agents can still deliver them into indefinite debt bondage. But student debt can also endure for decades; employment prospects are more and more uncertain, while default is increasingly likely. A damaged credit score—from one or two delayed payments in the case of private student loans—will pose additional obstacles to finding work, since many employers consult the debt payment schedules of applicants to gauge their reliability. Ironically, one of the quickest ways for graduates to discharge their education debt is to find lucrative work in the finance industry, issuing the kind of high-interest loans that deliver more and more of their brethren into debt traps, or speculating on the kind of derivatives that can seem more like double-trouble to those whose assets are being gambled on.[7]

If the indenture analogy doesn't persuade you, there are other ways of deciding that education debt is an especially immoral kind of labor contract. Since it involves the capture of future wages, we could think of it as precocious wage theft. Creditors, after all, are allowed to book down-the-line earnings from their loans in the present, as if these assets already existed. This is how the contents of our future wage packets are spirited onto the creditor's balance sheet, decades in advance of their being paid out. Yet another way of approaching student debt is to see it as an unauthorized tax collected by the government and the finance sector on behalf of the ultimate beneficiaries of a highly educated workforce. According to this analysis, debt interest is a tithe on our capacity to finance our training for employment that will unduly create wealth for the 1 percent.

Whether you accept the indenture analogy, or prefer one of these variants, when student debt is analyzed as a labor arrangement, it is difficult to avoid concluding that it is a particularly degraded one, far removed from the ethical tidiness of a fair contract. When viewed as a hallmark of a creditocracy, the labor implications of student debt are markedly dire. A society that might once have been distinguished by its capacity to attend to human welfare is rapidly transitioning to one driven by financial debtfare, where the majority are borrowing money, either for bare subsistence, or simply to make themselves acceptable to employers. Under such circumstances, it's no surprise to see a renewed interest in the "Human Capital" contracts first proposed by Milton Friedman and other neoliberal economists in the 1970s. In the spirit of these contracts, ex-Citigroup CEO Vikram Pandit and other start-up entrepreneurs are now looking to pay for the education of selected students in return for a percentage of their future earnings. If this is the future of higher education, it will be one where students will have to curry favor with their wealthy sponsors before they can even enroll in college. Of course, only those with high-earnings potential need apply. [8]

Workforce entrants, especially the college-educated, have always had to prepare themselves for employability. But an ever-greater share of their wages now goes to servicing the debts taken on to meet the basic mental and physical requirements demanded for modern work. These requirements include the direct fiscal burden of maintaining the kind of health profile favored by employers, which increasingly means items like gym membership fees (more or less obligatory for a huge slice of those under forty), more costly nutrition (because an affordable American diet of processed food makes people sick), along with preventive medicine (and other therapies to reduce stress). None of these are typically covered by health insurance, but all are now considered essential to maintaining the requisite mind-body balance for a well-tempered knowledge worker. Add on the costs of upskilling—the given wisdom that everyone now needs a master's degree (for which very little financial aid is usually available), not just a bachelor's, in order to compete for decent employment in the knowledge economy. And throw in the costs of self-support during at least one unpaid internship as the price of entry into any line of work that requires a college credential.

The time and the resources expended on all of these basic needs are more and more perceived as a hedge (in the language of financial instruments) against falling below the threshold of employability in the decades to come. I can hardly blame any of my students for adopting this calculating outlook, as they often do, though it is perfectly consistent with the mentality of a financialized society, which has exhausted its capacity for profit-taking in the present and resorts to circulating ever more paper claims on the future.[9] In the short term, they are encouraged to forestall the plight of graduate insolvency by majoring in market-friendly disciplines. For those unwilling to compromise their education in this way, the emerging pattern is to put more gratifying career paths on hold for several years, and therefore risk abandoning them, until they have paid off their loans through employment options that are much less desirable to them. Getting caught in the limbo of precarious labor or underemployment—the royal road to default—usually resolves the quandary, one way or another.

WORKING FOR NOTHING?

In June 2013, the official U.S. unemployment rate stood at 7.6 percent, with labor underutilization rates at 14.3 percent, and climbing. The "real" rate of unemployment was much higher, because the prolonged duration of the recession meant that millions were no longer counted under the Bureau of Labor Statistics category of those who are available or looking for work; after twelve months, they drop off the roster. By the end of the summer, the labor force participation rate had dropped to its lowest level in thirty-five years. In austerity-squeezed countries like Italy, Spain, and Greece, official youth unemployment levels were as high as 42 percent, 56 percent, and 65 percent respectively, with suicides on the rise. Most of the new jobs being created in the recession continue to be in sectors like restaurants, retail trade, and temporary help—among the lowest-paying positions, and the least likely to offer benefits and job security.

At the same time, we have seen the proliferation of unpaid, or token-wage, work. Indeed, a cynic might well conclude that "working for nothing" is the latest high-growth boomlet. In almost every sector, versions of the compensation-free work profile are flourishing. Some of these are new, and are occurring as part of the ongoing transfer of work to digital platforms. Others are upgrades of existing patterns (more intensive wage theft and use of prison labor), or they entail the conversion of formerly paid positions to unpaid ones, as is the case with internships. Still others rest on the industrial uptake of "working for exposure" as a normative career mentality for youth in particular. Can this upsurge of unpaid labor help explain the gulf between record corporate profits and high rates of underemployment? And what role does the personal debt-financing of education play in making this unrewarded or discounted labor available?

Two of the reasons for the gap between high earnings and joblessness seem to be beyond dispute. Corporations are still moving their operations offshore, especially jobs in high-skilled sectors where the largest savings in labor costs can be secured. In addition, these offshore activities allow them to dodge U.S. taxes by parking their profits overseas. A second explanation rests on increased productivity. Employees have been pressed by the stiff threat of layoffs, either to work harder and longer for the same paycheck or to take a cut in wages. A third reason—and this is the unfamiliar quantum—is the growing reliance on new kinds of unpaid labor to supplement the balance sheet of employers that are canny enough to harvest it. Conclusive proof of this footprint is not so easy to muster but the strong anecdotal record and the available documented evidence suggest it is large enough to be substantively significant.

Here are some of the more obvious areas where employers have been taking advantage of the worst employment market (and the weakest jobs recovery) since the 1930s. In each case, the violations of fair labor standards are magnified by an underlying condition of indebtedness:

- In the realm of digital work, a huge variety of unpaid labor is being extracted from sources such as the following: the establishment of free online media content as an industrial norm (taking a predictable toll on the pay scales of all kinds of professional writing and arts); extensive data mining from social media platforms like Facebook, Google, and Twitter, most often without the conscious knowledge of users; e-lance programs, like Amazon's Mechanical Turk, which allocate micro-tasks that may take no more than a few minutes to perform; crowdsourcing as an industrial principle; and a host of other sophisticated digital techniques (usually involving personalized algorithms) for extracting rents from users/participants. These are all forms of "distributed labor," and they use the Internet to mobilize the spare processing power of a widely dispersed multitude of discrete individuals. None of these arrangements comes close to any definition of nonstandard employment used by the Bureau of Labor Statistics, yet they are sources of sizable revenue to the knowledge firms, like Google or Facebook, which are posting sky-high profits, and showing equally astronomical earnings-to-payroll ratios. Facebook's earnings in the third quarter of 2013 were almost $2 billion, yet it employed no more than 5,000 employees. Google reported Q3 earnings of almost $15 billion, with an estimated 30,000 employees. These are extraordinary ratios, by any historical standards, presenting a seductive model for twenty-first-century capitalists to emulate.

Unpaid or under-compensated digital work affects all income and skill levels, from routine micro-tasking to high-concept livelihoods, but the biggest rewards for exploiting it are extracted from the creative sector of the economy. The more interesting and challenging a conceptual task is, the more likely it will be done for free by those willing to donate their time. Traditionally, creative work entails a good deal of volunteer, or discount, labor in return for job gratification. In recent years, as the uber-flexible creative has become the model neoliberal worker, this kind of sacrificial labor, which is often described as self-exploitation, has become an industrial principle, especially in deregulated, freelancing sectors where precarious employment is the norm.[10] Yet the personal debt burden associated with this kind of workforce has not been fully acknowledged. The self-training of these employees in typically creative fields—arts, design, writing, performance, architecture—often entails much higher levels of student debt than in sectors with standard employment profiles. These employees not only offer their labor at a discount; their availability also comes at a higher personal cost, because they have pledged these discounted wages in advance to the creditor through taking on high levels of education debt.

- Internships are no longer a rite of passage into the professional service sector; they have become near-obligatory in almost every white-collar or no-collar niche of the economy. In many cases, they are becoming a terminal limbo, not unlike the time spent by some graduate students in teaching, which is no longer a term of apprenticeship, but, practically speaking, the end of their teaching career. In the last few years, unpaid internships have become the norm, especially for women (paid positions are disproportionately occupied by males), and according to one 2011 estimate, cumulatively provide a $2 billion subsidy to employers in the U.S. alone.[11] As the market for internships develops, these unpaid positions are being openly sold, with the more sought-after placements generating substantial profits for middlemen and employers alike, amplifying the subsidy. Many, if not most, of these internships

Check for $2 billion subsidy to employers for unpaid internships, May Day, 2012 (courtesy Ross Perlin)

are off-the-books—they are neither counted nor recorded in any official estimates of labor activity. So, too, they are likely to magnify household debt. After all, a large portion of internships are undertaken for college credit, and so, in the U.S. at least, they will probably be debt-financed. Most of the others are all-but-compulsory adjuncts of the collegiate quest for credentials. Inevitably, some of these stints can only be borne by taking on more debt. The phenomenon of taking out loans simply to survive an unremunerated internship is more and more common.

- Wage theft has become a massive source of free labor for employers who routinely violate wages and hours laws, either by denying employees backpay, refusing to pay overtime, pocketing tips, paying below the minimum wage, or by demanding off-the-clock hours.[12] In 2008, at the onset of the recession, the National Employment Law Center estimated that, on average, low-wage workers (predominantly women and minorities) were losing 15 percent of their annual income to wage theft in one form or another.[13] In the years since then, and especially in economic sectors which rely heavily on migrant and immigrant labor, these illegal practices have become chronic. Downward pressure on the job market and stepped-up surveillance of immigrants has emboldened employers to deny pay to the more vulnerable members of their workforce. The rapid spread of tipping, from restaurant service to all kinds of in-person retail service jobs, is a recent innovation on the employers' efforts to pass on labor costs to customers. Once established as acceptable in a workplace, this practice becomes a legal rationale for paying the sub-minimum wage that many states set for tipped employees (as low as $2.13/hour by federal law).

Wage theft is not just a gratuity for employers but also for the lenders that prey on the unbanked. These predominantly low-income earners are increasingly forced to pay fees simply to access the cash-value of their paychecks. The multitude of check cashers, pawners, payday lenders, and other sharks in the poverty business are committing a form of wage theft from people who are denied the full fruits of their labor because they cannot be members of a mainstream bank. According to one estimate, the working poor pay an effective surcharge of about $30 billion a year for the financial products they consume on Loan Alley, and more than twice that if you include subprime credit cards, subprime auto loans, and subprime mortgages.[14]

- The pressure of import prices and recessionary drops in consumer demand has led employers to seek out sharply discounted prison labor in ever greater quantities. The use of convicts in manufacturing and services has also been amplified by the decision of many state legislatures to outsource prisoners to private penitentiaries. As a result of the Prison Industries Act, pushed into law under the powerful auspices of the American Legislative Exchange Council (ALEC), an estimated one million inmates are now tasked at sub-minimum wages, and their labor is secured by the kind of disciplining of conduct that could not be enforced on the outside. In addition, prison industry employers are allowed to deduct, from the meager wages on offer and from the sale of goods produced, the charges they set for room and board, family support, and other costs. Convict labor, the scourge of the nineteenth-century penal South, is back with a vengeance in some states.[15] In others, small-time debtors are increasingly detained for failure to make monthly payments, and while they typically face jail time (and not incarceration), it may only be a matter of time before they are sent to prison to pay off their debts through an inmate labor program.

- Student debt itself, as I have suggested, is a form of precocious wage theft, but avoidance of it also has a significant labor impact. A sizable portion of the academic curriculum has long been taught by graduate employees, looking for alternatives to the debt-financing of their studies. But campuses are now increasingly run on the back of their cheap undergraduate workforce. On many campuses, most of the clerical, landscaping, catering, and housekeeping duties are now performed by students trying to stave off taking on even more loans. In college towns, a variety of employers will take advantage of this desperation by treating the student body as a reserve army of cheap, temporary labor.[16]

- Last, but not least, contestant volunteering has transformed many sectors of the entertainment industries into an amateur talent show, with jackpot riches for a few winners and peanuts for everyone else. The talent show/reality TV model has now become an industry standard, undercutting pay scales in all occupations. Given the powerful influence of popular entertainers over youth, the central principle of "working for exposure" is becoming a normative career mentality, with uncertain economic consequences. Young people have accepted that this is the way of the world, and that they can only get ahead by offering their self-fashioned labor in advance and gratis, in hopes of being noticed and favored. For a generation at least, the wages of industrialization have been replaced by the affective currency of attention and prestige. Under these circumstances, toil and effort buys the equivalent of a lottery ticket in the livelihood sweepstakes.

Is this new norm a significant shift beyond the more traditional use of "casting" as an entry model for the entertainment workforce? If so, it may be because working for exposure is now regarded as part of the necessary upfront costs of stacking a resume for a livelihood based on gainful recognition. Just as student debts are taken on as a hedge against unemployability in the future, the donor labor given over to personal skill-building is a levy extracted in advance by industry employers, a gift of time and resources that employers would otherwise have had to absorb for job training, or the polishing of work personalities. But unlike membership dues, paid in advance to join an organization, there are no guarantees of benefits for the users. The only sure thing here is the extraction of free labor for employers who will take advantage of it.

One of the distinctive features of the foregoing survey of "working for nothing" is that these practices are by no means confined to traditionally low-wage sectors. Indeed, some of the fastest developing trends in unpaid labor can be found in sectors of high-reward toil, especially in the creative industries, where amateur effort to win a niche in the attention economy can result in "blockbuster hits," but where there seem to be very few yardsticks any more for judging what fair labor is. Any attempt to draw a crisp equation between work and pay is increasingly fruitless. Nor do most of the losing "contestants" in this economy experience their thwarted endeavor as a form of exploited labor.

The systemic shift toward "temping," which characterized the last three decades of job casualization, is being succeeded by an even more tenuous contractual relationship. Some of the new work arrangements, especially the digital micro-tasking, leave little trace of employment, and certainly nothing to implicate an employer in any legal or regulated network of obligations. On the one hand, they move the definition of a "job" much closer to its etymological source—a discrete "lump," or "piece," of work that exists only for the duration of its fulfillment. On the other hand, and insofar as some of them are driven by the self-promotion of ordinary, unpaid individuals, the rewards are more typical of a preindustrial era, when the careful nurturing of attention from wealthy and powerful names or institutions were sources of considerable value and social mobility. They also evoke a time when the relationship of the indebted to creditors was not only more intimate but also more liable to penal hardship when it turned sour.

At best, compensation in the present is not stolen so much as postponed to some indeterminate point in the future. In this respect, the worker should not be regarded as the one in debt; in reality, it is the employer who owes. As Michael Denning points out, the underlying principle of wage labor is that employees are in the position of being creditors, because "every day we make an interest-free loan of our labor power to our employers":

> "Every time one takes a new job, one is reminded that you must support yourself without pay for the first day, week, or month. For one of the most curious aspects of the fictitious commodity the temp agencies call "manpower" is that it is one of the few commodities that is consumed before it is paid for. With most commodities, one pays and then enjoys. There are a handful of quotidian exceptions, like the restaurant meal—hence the deeply frowned-upon act of skipping out on a check. We do often get to use a commodity before paying for it, but these are always seen as a loan by the retailer or by a third party like a credit card issuer. Only in the case of wage labor is the commodity used up before it is paid for; "everywhere," Marx noted in an aside in *Capital*,

"the worker allows credit to the capitalist." Perhaps the most revealing metaphor we have of this time warp is that, in the rare instances where someone is paid before working, it is called an "advance," a usage that goes back in English to the early eighteenth century.[17]"

BODY AND SOUL

When they are pushing for the adoption of austerity policies, deficit hawks often make a point of invoking inter-generational justice—it is unjust to pass on large public debts to our children and grandchildren. But public debts are nowhere near as threatening or as burdensome as the austerians have depicted. Arguably, it would be more unfair to hand down to the next generation a severely damaged democracy, in which every household activity is a market opening for creditors to extract revenue. When a society converts its key social needs into a pool of economic rents to be collected by profiteers, then it is not only legitimate to refuse debts incurred in the process, as I have argued; it may also the only way of ensuring that the future will be different for our children. Borrowing is always an act of renouncing the future, especially when compound interest rates swallow up great chunks of it. Loans are pledges of our time and labor in advance. At what point does the aggregate sum of all these promises choke off the routes toward unbidden versions of the future? When the cost of a debt exceeds the value of the underlying asset, we are in a condition of negative equity, according to the language of finance. What is the equivalent for a liberal society? When democracy itself defaults?

During the Cold War, Western democracies sought to deliver an incrementally improved future for the majority. This promise rested on the guarantee of universal healthcare, and so most of these countries established a national system of medical provision. Earlier forms of social insurance, in Britain and Germany, were instituted to stave off socialism, buy workers' political allegiance, or stem the advance of their trade unions. In the postwar U.S., the Truman administration's efforts to promote national health-care were effectively scuttled by anti-communist sloganeering on the part of the medical industry and its legislative allies. Unions were also anxious about losing their highly-prized capacity to win social benefits on behalf of their members. Yet, in the absence of a universal government-run program, it was the flourishing of union-negotiated health care benefits that cushioned workers from the full impact of health care costs and became such a central component of the post-war social contract. In order to compete, in an era of relatively full employment, nonunion employers were also obliged to offer a steadily growing umbrella of benefits, none of it dependent on debt-financing. In this way, the union wage also became a social wage for a much larger portion of the population. For many recipients, employee health benefits were prized more than the expanding pay packet—healthcare insurance was often the one good reason to stay in a humdrum job.

However much it may have been kept afloat by consumer credit, the creation of a relatively stable middle class with rising fiscal expectations and with some promise of physical and mental security in old age was the pinnacle achievement of the

American century. But this attainment has steadily eroded over the last forty years. Healthcare costs have risen almost as fast as the net price of college education, and the surge of medical debt, even for those who have private insurance coverage, seems unstoppable. When judged by any of the metrics of public health, the U.S. spends vastly more on medical treatment, and gets fewer results, than any other industrialized nation. By 2011, these costs accounted for almost 18 percent of GDP (Netherlands was the nearest rich country, at 12 percent), and will consume a fifth of the economy by 2021, according to government estimates.[18] Between 1950 and 2011, real GDP per capita in the U.S. grew at an average of 2.0 percent per year, while real national health care expenditures per capita grew at 4.4 percent per year.[19] The gap between the two rates of growth is unsustainable. Nor is there any reason to believe that the overall costs (and the debts) will be reined in by the healthcare reforms passed by the Obama administration in 2010, since the changes will almost certainly stimulate expenditure growth. By comparison, a single-payer, national health system would slice costs, boost health outcomes, and abolish the crushing burden of medical debt (almost non-existent in the rest of the industrialized world) by spreading the risk appropriately.

Obamacare will almost certainly reduce debts for many of the previously uninsured. But its mandates may also help to enlarge the web of debt by swelling the ranks of the "underinsured," who will now include those choosing the bronze plans, with the lowest premiums, covering only 60 percent of enrollee costs. The latter may well seek out more treatment than they did before they were insured, but they will be unable to pay in full their hospital bills and drug costs because the "actuarial values" estimated by insurers condemn them in advance to a regime of borrowing to make up the difference. For the private sector, Obamacare guarantees that profits will continue to be lavish, not only for the medical industry, but also for the financial institutions that collect on patients' debts, set credit ratings for the hospitals, and supply the loans to keep the market-driven complex in business. As the numbers of uninsured dwindle, the case for charitable patient care, which is relatively debt-free, will also wear thin; public and community hospitals are already being pushed out of business as the private, and increasingly monopolistic, giants reinforce their dominance.[20]

One of the symptoms of living in a creditocracy is that the future appears to have been forfeited. No longer cherished as a time when we will have earned the right to be more free, the future is increasingly foreshadowed as a long drawn-out period, now stretching well into old age, when we will be hard put to service our debts. For some time now, the finance industry's sights have been set on privatizing Medicare and Social Security, the only pillars of Cold War social insurance left standing. In 1980, 40 percent of the American workforce enjoyed traditional defined-benefit pensions. More than half of these have since been converted into risky 401(k) plans, feeding directly into Wall Street's profits. Because they shift risk away from the employer and on to the individual, corporations are stripping away benefits from employment contracts as fast they can draw them up. Taking their cue from the private sector, politicians and state managers increasingly push for deep cuts in the pension obligations of public employees.[21] The same pattern of decline applies to employer-provided health insurance; those who still enjoy it are paying much more for the premiums, and getting less coverage in return. One outcome is the steady rise in the percentage of personal bankruptcies driven by medical debt. Only 8 percent in 1981, it had ballooned to 50 percent in 2001, and was topping 62 percent by 2007. Research on that pattern, by Elizabeth Warren and other Harvard colleagues, found that 78 percent of those filing in 2007 had medical insurance at the start of their illness, including 60.3 percent who had private coverage.[22] Nor is there evidence to suggest that Obamacare will reduce medical bankruptcies—in fact, there was no appreciable decrease when the same kind of healthcare program was introduced in Massachusetts under Governor Mitt Romney.[23]

Almost as telling are the numbers of currently employed who are forced to take early withdrawals from their retirement accounts to pay medical debts, even when such an action entails steep penalties.[24] This amounts to self-cannibalization for those whose capacity to keep body and soul together in the present has been decimated by for-profit healthcare. Pledging future wages is an implicit part of any formal debt contract, but in this instance, maintaining physical comfort in the present requires us to concede the means to do so in the years to come. Ensuring that the elderly can survive after they outlast their capacity to earn a living wage is a core principle of a humane society, and it is far more important, as a test of generational justice, than keeping public debts in check. When we are forced to surrender that long-term assurance in order to stay alive in the short term, then the right to life, if not liberty, is under threat.

That is why David Blacker includes healthcare along with education debt in his definition of "existential debt"—"a kind of debt from which it is impossible to separate one's very continued existence." Existential debts, he argues, "that have been accrued against one's very being are *ipso facto* intolerable for any kind of just and democratic society because they attach too comprehensively and exert such excessive control over individuals as they move through life."[25] In the case of student and medical debts, the proprietary assets—and the ones against which these debts are securitized—are raw, component parts of ourselves, not external commodities like cars and houses. Indeed, it is because they are so intrinsic to maintaining life and life's options that these very modern American debts are often compared to conditions of feudal servitude and peonage, where the constraining bonds are lifelong, inescapable, and determinative of physical survival. Recognizing such debts as illegitimate should not simply be a prelude to individual bargaining over the terms of repayment. Their repudiation, and, ultimately, their abolition, is surely a pressing matter for any society that values human freedom.

HOW SHOULD LABOR RESPOND?

Because student debt is non-dischargeable, and there is no statute of limitations on federal loans, it has assumed the air of inescapability. Indeed, many borrowers speak about their student debt as if it were a kind of life sentence. Accordingly, the compulsion to service the debt is deepened by a strong retributive underpinning, and it is reinforced by the personal shame and guilt that accompanies default. While this moralism eats away at the debtor's disposition, it is all the more essential to the creditors' ability to collect. That is why the prospect of large-scale debt forgiveness presents such a dilemma to elites. Without mass household relief, the consumer economy is stagnant at best, but extending forgiveness would corrode the all-important payback morality on which a creditocracy depends for its collection efforts. In the early twentieth century, Henry Ford and other industrialists concluded that factory wages had to be raised in order to give birth to the consumer society. After all, workers had to be able to afford the Model Ts they were making. In retrospect, this principle seems like common sense, but, at the time, raising wages went entirely against the grain of capitalist habit. In that same spirit, today's economic managers may well have to entertain debt reduction programs in order to facilitate the reentry of debtors into the marketplace of big-ticket consumer life. But doing so will run the risk of eroding payback morality. The moral injunction to pay back is the disciplinary backbone of today's finance capitalism in the same way as wage controls were for industrial capitalists like Ford, but overriding it, even temporarily, would pose a much greater threat to long-term Wall Street profits.

Besides, it is worth recalling that Ford's five-dollars-a-day wage was not enough to buy his cars. External financing was needed, and it was these auto loans, not higher factory wages, that jumpstarted the consumer revolution and the industrial culture of personal lending that supported it. The wage raise was more of a barefaced gambit to stave off unions, and workers' access to this expanded pay packet depended on their observance of Ford's own moral standards of thrift, sobriety, and other (bourgeois) family values, as overseen by his firm's Sociology Department. This pattern of intrusion into workers' personal lives was extended during the 1920s heyday of welfare capitalism, built to compete against the appeal of socialist alternatives. When unions finally won their right to operate within industry workplaces they effectively took over responsibility for the moral discipline of the workforce. Union officials were tasked with ensuring that the life habits of their members did not obstruct the high workplace productivity demanded in return for scheduled increases in the union wage.

In the nineteenth century, the moral strictures that governed the industrial work ethic required a small army of advocates—preachers, educators, and business leaders—to promote them with ample zeal and conviction.[26] Over time, labor advocates fashioned their own version of the dignity of labor, though more to instill worker pride than to motivate intensified work effort. But what is the equivalent of the gospel of work for a financialized economy?

What self-serving humbug do creditors need borrowers to buy in to? Payback morality requires exponents to pound home the virtues of debtors who keep their promises, and also the shortcomings of those who cannot. The shame and guilt that stigmatizes (and is internalized by) the defaulter today echoes with the condescension trained on the ne'er-do-well shiftless of the factory era, who were disparaged for not being able to find or hold down a job. There is a good deal of continuity between these two regimes of proselytizing, reinforcing the historical intimacy between labor and debt that I have been sketching in this chapter. But, unlike the nineteenth century sermonizers of the gospel of work, Wall Street moguls are hardly in a position to preach about ethics. In the public mind, they probably command less respect than Mafia bosses, their companions in extortion, and, unlike the latter, are rarely depicted in a positive light in popular culture.

Labor advocates today have every reason to push aside the thick bluster of Wall Street moralism and promote debt cancellation as a cause for working people. As household debt mounted during the 1990s, even Alan Greenspan had cause to acknowledge, albeit approvingly, the chilling impact on labor militancy—workers were much less inclined to go out on strike if they had debt payments to make.[27] Under the hammer of today's austerity, municipal and sovereign debt is being manipulated to extract deep concessions from public employees—teachers, transit workers, firefighters, police, letter carriers, and other urban service workforces. Right-wing governors, beginning with Wisconsin's Scott Walker, have seized the opportunity of the debt crisis to break the strength of public sector unions in particular, by introducing right-to-work legislation. Some of these unions were active participants in the Occupy protests-especially the Transit Workers Union in New York City—while the leaders of others, like the ILWU dockworkers in Oakland, looked the other way when their members engaged in wildcat actions along with Occupy activists. Public sector unions have also been in the forefront of Europe's massive anti-austerity strikes, openly fighting to preserve their rights as well as their jobs. In some cases, debt audits are proving to be a useful tool to unionists who want to fight back in more innovative ways; the audits can expose the dubious underpinnings of public debts and also the machinations by which these debts are being used to punish employees.

When the legendary union organizer Tony Mazzochi founded the Labor Party in 2000, its primary platform plank was a Free Higher Ed campaign, aimed at restoring to tertiary education the levels of state support provided during the Cold War decades. As Adolph Reed, a leading advocate for the campaign, put it, "This program isn't pie in the sky. It has a clear precedent in living memory. The GI Bill paid full tuition and fees, as well as a living-wage stipend, for nearly eight million returning World War II veterans. We've done it before, we can do it again, and this time for everyone."[28] Given the economic plight of today's increasingly strapped working families, the appeal of tuition-free education is self-evident. Who would not want their children to have a college education that did not encumber them financially for a lifetime?

In July 2012, Rich Trumka, AFL-CIO president, made the following comments to student activists: "Your generation's struggle for jobs—for quality jobs—with fair wages and good benefits, so that those of you who have student debt can have the ability to pay it down and have the opportunity to live the life you want: the ability to get married, to raise a family if you want to, to start a business, to fight for the causes you believe in, and to leave a stronger America for the generations that follow you—that struggle is the struggle of the labor movement, and that struggle is also my struggle."[29] While a notable statement of solidarity, Trumka's declaration of principle was a far cry from the much stronger Labor Party position that free education is a right and a social good.

The U.S. trade union movement has a rich history of opposing debt bondage. In its infancy, it pushed for free public education along with the abolition of imprisonment for debt, and, in the late nineteenth century, it fought for the right to be paid in cash, rather than in the employers' favored currency of company scrip. In the 1920s, the movement established alternative, nonprofit financial institutions—including the once mighty Amalgamated Bank, and many mutual credit unions—while pioneering the spread of the cooperative housing movement that provided affordable apartments for members. Today, it is responding to the steady rise of nontraditional employment by welcoming innovative modes of alt-labor organizing, not only through independent workers' centers and initiatives like the AFL-CIO's own Working America, designed for workers who cannot unionize, but also in organizations like the

National Domestic Workers Alliance, Freelancers Union, Retail Action Project, Restaurant Opportunities Center, Coalition of Immokalee Workers, Model Alliance, Fast Food Forward, Intern Labor Rights, WashTech, Brandworkers, and Taxi Workers Alliance. These fledgling alternatives to single-employer unions are a necessary step to rebuilding power of labor in a restructured and de-financialized economy. But the labor movement should also take a more central role in the push to restore free public education, the single most effective way of bringing debt relief to working households.

THE LOST GENERATION?

It can hardly be disregarded that the amassment of student debt has occurred in tandem with the sharp rise of precarious employment over the last two decades. Just when creditors are relying more and more on returns from future wages, the prospect of secure employment and steady income has dissolved for a large portion of student debtors. Oftentimes, the most indebted graduates are the ones confronted with a volatile gigs-based economy, where they must assume all the market risks of the freelancer, and are forced to stay afloat by piecing together or juggling disparate streams of revenue. During the dotcom era, cheerleading for the virtues of this precarious work profile took the form of glorification of "free agents"; these liberated souls were boldly choosing extreme self-employment over the "risk-averse constraints" of job security in the Old Economy.[30] A subsequent crusade in the mid-2000s to trumpet the "human capital" of urban creative workers helped to further glamorize high-risk livelihoods with lumpy income sources and debt-dependent credentials.[31] When employers began to mine the "working for nothing" vein in the recessionary years, they were building on the weak labor norms established by these two earlier barrages of propaganda for the cause of DIY employment.

The precarious character of most of this self-reliant labor is not an unlucky by-product of the knowledge economy, but more like its default condition. How does the acute uncertainty of precarious work sit with the promises made by elites about the fruits of a college education? High school students are repeatedly told that a college degree is the ticket to middle-class comfort, if not affluence, and a prerequisite for all the twenty-first century jobs that are in the pipeline. Given the ballooning costs of college attendance, it is hardly surprising when the outcome is measured as a return on investment. But how can the jobs economy accommodate graduates in a way that matches the promises? While it remains the case that job-seekers with a college degree will earn twice as much, on average, than those with a high school diploma, less than 30 percent of the U.S. jobs available actually do require a degree. By one estimate, almost half of employed U.S. college graduates are currently in jobs that require less than a four-year college education.[32] The general picture of supply and demand on the high-skill jobs landscape suggests an *overproduction* of college graduates. The resulting underemployment, at least for those who rationalize education in this way, begs to be interpreted as a massive waste of human capital.

One conclusion to take away from data like this is that the U.S. is more committed to the business of producing college graduates than it is to producing jobs for them. Just as if he were setting an industrial quota, Barack Obama promised, in his 2009 Address to the Joint Session of Congress, that "by 2020, America would once again have the highest-proportion of college graduates in the world." This goal was introduced in response to further evidence that the nation was falling behind others in its output: "While the United States ranks ninth in the world in the proportion of young adults enrolled in college, we've fallen to sixteenth in the world in our share of certificates and degrees awarded to adults ages 25-34—lagging behind Korea, Canada, Japan, and other nations."[33]

In that same speech, the president also committed his administration to creating high-skill jobs, many of them through the stimulus impact of the American Recovery and Reinvestment Act. But the following year, the White House turned the government's giant economic lever away from stimulus and toward austerity, all but guaranteeing an even greater mismatch between the output of graduates and the availability of skills-appropriate jobs. National industrial policy might still be aimed at boosting the numbers of those with degrees, but it would not be delivering the kind of "high road" jobs needed to absorb the surplus graduate population. In fact, the institutionalization of degree growth targets further fueled a higher education boom that has been a bonanza for the creditor class, whether through profits from student lending or from the capital-intensive building plans that almost every college has undertaken as part of its own market-driven growth. As long as the financial gravy train was still running at high speed, there was little reason for investors to put their money elsewhere.

From the mid-1990s, graduates were forced to cope with the onerous burden of student debt, but the growing mismatch between the shiny promises of New Economy jobs and the grisly realities of the employment market has taken a deeper toll on the "millennials." The widespread dissatisfaction of overqualified employees with humdrum service industry jobs was bad enough. Graduating into the worst labor market since the Great Depression under a mountain of debt has poured even more salt on the wound. So it is hardly surprising when the predicament of debtors gets framed in generational terms. Lampooned in the popular media as work-shy, these "boomerang" offspring and underemployed "adultescents" have not been slow in fighting back. One prominent example is *Generation Debt*, Anya Kamenetz's penetrating 2006 analysis of the economic obstacles, and the condescension confronting her newly graduated peers. In the course of her commentary, Kamenetz describes her sympathy for the arguments of deficit hawks like Pete Peterson who inveigh against bequeathing a crushing legacy of national debt to younger generations. As a liberal, she is fully aware of the conservative credentials and goals of austerians like Peterson, but she nonetheless acknowledges the force of her generation's resentment at baby boomers who are oblivious to the consequences of ignoring the national deficit. These beneficiaries of the GI Bill seem unwilling to share the sacrifices being laid at the door of her generation. "The generational divide," Kamenetz concludes, "becomes a class divide" when we consider who is paying the price for Social Security and other retirement securities that may not be around for her and her peers.

Full-court media pressure from Peterson's Fix the Debt campaign promoted the fallacy that baby boomers were selfishly "eating their young" by protecting retirees' right to the few components of the welfare net left intact. From this perspective, attempts to preserve Medicare, Social Security, and public pension plans were more damaging than the plundering of the economy by the Wall Street tycoons who are spokespersons for Fix the Debt. Somehow, the real injustice being perpetrated in recessionary America was a "war on youth" being collectively waged by an abstract group of sixty-five year olds![34] Framing these government programs as boomer "entitlements," which younger workers cannot afford to fund, is cut from exactly the same cloth as the right-wing use of that label to slash support for other welfare rights and programs. At a time when the starkest resource grab is the upward wealth redistribution to the 1 percent, it's easy to see why conservatives would look to promote generational conflict as a smokescreen. Payroll taxes that fund these programs are a sideshow when the heaviest burdens on young people are the runaway costs of for-profit health care and debt-financed education. It is cruelty beyond measure to suggest that the solution to youth impoverishment is to sacrifice their only future prospect of security in the form of social insurance.

That is not to say there is no generational component to the pattern of debt. There is no question that young people are more disadvantaged economically than their parents or grandparents (though the chronic inequalities of gender, race, and class still weigh more than generational differences).[35] They may have iPhones and Facebook accounts, but, on average, they have less access to affordable social goods, fewer income prospects, a lower standard of living, and less chance of social mobility than their immediate forebears. So, too, their high debt load means that the finance industry has captured them early on as lifelong revolvers. Plied with credit from high school onward, not only have their future wages been claimed, but every corner of their lives, including those Facebook accounts, has been mined for profit.

But the perception of unfair victimization and of having been sold out as a generation has also energized and mobilized young people, especially those who participated in, or were influenced by, Occupy Wall Street. The Occupiers are drop-outs, but not in the way that traditional bohemians from the 1950s and 1960s were. The voluntary poverty of the latter was an act of Romantic identification. The bohemian was able to communicate, through dress, speech, and other expressions of lifestyle, that he or she had chosen to shun the comforts of affluence. Today's indie descendants of the bohemian counterculture continue to embrace conduct that breaks with parental norms, but, like their forebears, they cannot prevent their own substitute norms from being absorbed into the elastic fabric of the commercial marketplace. By contrast, wearing a sign that declares "I Owe $50,000" advertises something else—an inadvertent status from which there is no easy escape back into the world of middle-class amenities and self-satisfaction. Heavily indebted millennials have a different script to follow—resentment, refusal, and exit into non-capitalist economies.

Politicized student debtors may be a new kind of mass social actor. They are focused on identifying the profiteers and the various forms of state violence—laws, courts, police, and legislators in the pockets of bankers—that protect the interests of the creditor class. Because their debts are tethered to their future ability to work, they are labor activists in all but name, and, in this respect, they are in a long line of descent. So, too, their debt burden is invariably shared with, and is connected to the economic obligations of, their parents and other family members. Indeed, as the household debt burden increasingly shifts onto the elderly, largely as a result of parents and grandparents co-signing student loans, the prospects for intergenerational protest will multiply. Far from a "war against youth," the more likely prognosis is for a "war with youth," against the creditocracy.

HONORING CLIMATE DEBTS

At the height of the Congressional feeding frenzy over the "fiscal cliff," austerity hawks coined a new label—"debt deniers." Minted to belittle lawmakers who were opposed to social spending cuts prompted by the cynical manipulation of federal debt, it was subsequently used as Tea Party ammunition during the government shutdown over raising the debt ceiling in the fall of 2013. The label was a savvy way for the deficit scolds to turn the tables on Democrats who had gotten traction out of depicting the GOP as hopelessly afflicted by "climate denial." Whose heads were buried deeper in the sand? The anti-science crowd on the Right or the folks on the other side of the aisle for whom ballooning public debt was not a clear and present danger requiring drastic spending cuts?

Not that there was any real equivalence between the two charges. After all, economics, unlike climatology, is not a science, and there is nothing approaching a consensus about the fiscal wisdom of running large government debts, especially if they are backed by the still almighty dollar. Nor was it surprising to learn that the phrase "debt denial" was cooked up by Fix the Debt, the CEO-backed campaign that lobbies Congress to slice Social Security, Medicare, and Medicaid and funnel more tax breaks to corporations. The charge quickly became part of the fighting arsenal of candidates running for office. Just as the long-standing no-tax pledge of Grover Norquist was finally losing its sway over the GOP faithful, debt-fixing fundamentalism was becoming the new article of faith among the conservative ranks.

Conspicuously missing from the grandstanding on Capitol Hill was any mention of the debt owed by high carbon emitters like the U.S. to those heavily impacted by climate change in the poor countries of the world. Climate debt, which is financially complex but morally simple, is not yet part of the political lexicon in the U.S., and winning recognition for its validity is still an uphill struggle. Full acknowledgment of this debt obligation entails facing up to some uncomfortable truths—the dependency, for example, of high standards of American living on sacrifice, immiseration, and ecological ruin elsewhere. As a result, denial about climate debt runs high even among those who readily accept the consensus about the grievous threat posed by climate change. If it is a legitimate debt—and therefore one that we really do have to honor—then who, exactly, is responsible for meeting the obligations, and how are they to be calculated? Just as climate debts are a product of uneven development, surely the liabilities for repayment must be fairly distributed, within, as well as between, nations? And, in the event of full repayment, who can guarantee that the benefits will reach the populations that need them most?

By 2013, the consensus about the climate threat included the world's leading international finance institutions. Speaking at the World Economic Forum in Davos, IMF director Christine Lagarde described climate change as "the greatest economic challenge of the twenty-first century," made a pitch for "green growth that respects environmental sustainability," and argued for "getting carbon pricing right and removing fossil fuel subsidies." Commenting on the release of a devastating 2012 World Bank report, *Turn Down the Heat*, its president Jim Yong Kim urged that "a 4°C warmer world can, and must be, avoided—we need to hold warming below 2°C," and "assume the moral responsibility to take action on behalf of future generations, especially the poorest."[1]

Indeed, both the IMF and the World Bank have fully acknowledged that the brunt of climate change's impact will be borne by some of the poorest populations in the world, further jeopardizing their prospects of sustainable development. But neither institution has made a point of encouraging, let alone pressing, rich nations to pay their climate debts to developing countries that have already felt the effects of climate change. Given their long history of delivering global South countries into a debt trap, it may be asking too much for the IMF or the World Bank to pay all that much attention when the creditor-debtor relationship is reversed, as it is under the terms of climate debt. "Denial" may be a weak characterization of the structural resistance at work here, but there is also no question that the disinclination to repay climate debts extends far beyond recalcitrant members of the international financial community.

The debt trap has been a familiar outcome of neoliberal policies, like structural adjustment, since the 1970s, but it builds directly on patterns established through centuries of colonial extraction. The annual payment imposed by the French government on Haiti, from 1825 to 1947, as compensation for slave-owners' lost "property," is the most striking example of how debt service is administered as a punishment and an instrument of control. The more predatory approach to sovereign debts flourishes today in the legal leeway granted to vulture funds (Donegal International, Elliott Management, FG Hemisphere). These are particularly venal private equity or hedge funds—considered pariahs even in the financial community—whose owners buy the distressed sovereign debt of defaulting countries at sharply reduced prices on the secondary market and then sue in London and New York courts to collect the full amount when the country's economy has recovered.

The piracy of these vulture funds is redolent of the resource exploitation of the South during the colonial era. Indeed, it is that historical pattern of plunder that most analysts hold responsible for the North's ecological debt to developing countries. The concept of "ecological debt" was first introduced by Chile's *Instituto de Ecologica Politica* in the lead-up to the 1992 Earth Summit in Rio de Janeiro. It was intended as a framework for discussing whether countries in the South should be responsible for repaying in full the external debts they had accumulated over the previous three decades. How did these debts to foreign creditors compare with the North's liabilities for environmental impacts from early colonization onward? Surely the South's claims as an eco-creditor were just as valid as the fiscal right of the North American and European banks to be repaid? Who owes what to whom? The ensuing debate within the Jubilee South movement about cancellation of "odious" and illegitimate debts imposed on poor countries was informed by this ecological backdrop, one with a much longer time line than the more recent postcolonial period of structural adjustment. Many argued that the obligation to repay the recent high-interest loans had to be weighed against moral and economic liabilities from the more distant past, and that any honest estimate of the balance of payments would lend itself to cancellation of all external debts.[2]

Even so, the full dimensions of ecological debt do not readily lend themselves to quantification. They range from the net pillage of resources through extractive industry and all of its associated pollution and biodiversity damage, to the loss of populations from the slave trade and colonial wars, and they extend to today's biopiracy of genetic resources from plants and agriculture.[3] While all of this damage is difficult to quantify, carbon debts *can* be measured more reliably, on the basis of atmospheric emissions estimates. It was this carbon-specific portion of the ecological obligation that emerged in the 2000s as the main vehicle for demanding repayment of what has come to be known today as climate debt. Not only is climate debt morally owed by the beneficiaries of carbon-rich industrialization, it can also be calculated with some degree of exactitude.

In fact, the exact share of responsibility for fossil fuel-derived CO_2 pollution—from 1750 onward—can be broken down, country by country. NASA climatologist James Hansen included such an itemization in a well-publicized 2008 letter to Australian prime minister Kevin Rudd, in support of a call for reducing that country's net emissions. According to Hansen's estimate, the historical carbon debt of the U.S. was 27.5 percent of the total, though the U.K.'s per capita obligation exceeded that of the U.S. ($33,307 and $31,035, respectively), with Germany and Australia clocking in at third and fourth ($27,856 and $24,265 per capita respectively).[4] Monetary estimates of carbon pollution are typically valued at $100 per ton of carbon dioxide—i.e. the cost of making wind power competitive in current energy markets. According to this scale of carbon pricing, the industrialized countries of the North all have net climate debts, with the U.S. topping the list at $9.7 trillion, followed by Germany ($2.3 trillion) and the U.K. ($2.1 trillion). The net climate creditors are led by India, at $6.5 trillion. Pushback against meeting the North's responsibilities is often expressed by pointing to the mercurial rise in emissions recorded by fast-growth economies in the South. China, for example, overtook the United States as the world's biggest producer of carbon dioxide in 2007. Yet assessments of historical carbon debt show China with a net climate credit of as much as $2.3 trillion.[5]

The belief in such rigorous measurements helped build confidence in the movement to hold the rich nations to account. Documented evidence that atmospheric global warming was already taking its toll on poor countries and their most marginal populations also bolstered the case for climate debt repayment. These impacts included the massive loss of fresh water through glacier, permafrost, and ice sheet melting; soil salinization and desertification; rainforest die-back; habitat degradation and coastal inundation; species mega-loss and reef erosion; and lower crop yields. As the case for climate justice entered the arena of international treaty-making, through the United Nations Framework Convention on Climate Change (UNFCCC) process, it was made, forcibly and dramatically, on behalf of populations whose very survival was threatened, most especially in the low-lying island states at risk of being entirely submerged. More than fifty developing nations joined with the Alliance of Small Island States and the Least Developed Countries group, representing forty-nine of the world's poorest nations, to push for repayment in one form or another.

The legal groundwork for such claims was laid in 1997 when the Kyoto Protocol institutionalized the concept of "common but differentiated responsibilities" between nations. The atmosphere is considered part of the biosphere commons, but the

Kyoto concession acknowledged that a few nations had already used up most of its sustainable carbon budget. Even so, climate activists did not fully take up the call for debt justice until the lead-up to the Copenhagen UNFCCC summit in 2008. In what was intended as a preemptive strike against any treaty-making that incorporated climate reparations, the U.S. State Department lead negotiator Todd Stern issued a statement before the summit rejecting the idea that the U.S. could be retroactively responsible for a problem that could not have been predicted. "For most of the two hundred years since the Industrial Revolution," Stern declared, "people were blissfully ignorant of the fact that emissions caused a greenhouse effect. It's a relatively recent phenomenon." Seen from this perspective, there would be a much narrower window for making repayment claims, on the basis of emissions since 1990, say, when a verifiable link between atmospheric CO_2 and climate change was established by the Intergovernmental Panel on Climate Change's (IPCC) first assessment. Arguably, the diminished time frame illustrates the perils of separating off the most quantifiable allotment of ecological debt—uneven carbon emissions—as the basis for negotiations. Nevertheless, none of the major carbon powers conceded even this more limited liability at the 2008 summit.

The dismal failure to agree on any binding emissions reductions at Copenhagen moved grassroots activists to pour their ideas and energies into the World People's Climate Summit held the following year in Cochabamba, Bolivia. This time, climate debt was front and center in the discussions among many of the working groups. The Climate Justice Tribunal group, in particular, envisaged "the creation of an International Tribunal of Climate and Environmental Justice that has the legally binding capacity to prevent, judge, and punish those states, companies, and individuals that pollute and cause climate change by their actions or omissions." Establishing bodies like this, with international jurisdiction and competence, was seen as a fair and autonomous response not only to the failure of representatives of the nation-state system to take appropriate action but also to the absence of any court for judging the ecological crimes of multilateral organizations and transnational corporations. By the end of the People's Summit, there was a consensus that the redistributive principles of climate justice were the most feasible framework for coordinating the work of a broad spectrum of social movement organizing. The final draft of the Cochabamba Declaration stated firmly that the North's repayment of the climate debt had to be "the basis for a just, effective, and scientific solution to climate change."

Of these three qualifiers, justice was the key contribution coming out of Cochabamba. After all, there are other kinds of solutions on the table that could plausibly be put forth as "effective" or "scientific." Large-scale geo-engineering schemes (such as seeding the world's oceans with iron, cloud whitening or space sunshading with sulfur aerosols to deflect solar radiation) might fall into either category, as might the fiscal mechanism of fully realized carbon markets ("privatization of the air"), or offset programs like the UN's REDD (Reducing Emissions from Deforestation and Forest Degradation) by which polluters can purchase carbon credits through rainforest conservation.[6] Each of these solutions might contribute to an overall reduction of the atmosphere's carbon load, but none of them proceed along democratic pathways. They are elite or technocratic options, crafted by "experts" without the consent or the participation of sovereign populations, let alone those most affected by climate change. Solutions like these entail no changes in the conduct of big polluters, and no enforcement of liabilities on the part of carbon-rich populations. Nor do they offer immediate relief for those suffering the impacts. Most of them carry a substantial degree of technical risk (whether in the form of catastrophic ecosystem damage or market failure), and all would reinforce existing patterns of inequality, magnifying the state of eco-apartheid that condemns those with an unfair share of the carbon budget to underdevelopment.

Other purely market-based solutions promise equally undemocratic outcomes. For example, advocates for green, or natural, capitalism tend to focus solely on the LOHAS (Lifestyles of Health and Sustainability) segment of consumer markets, which comprises 20 percent of the adult population of OECD countries. Marketing green gizmos to affluent populations who already have access to a range of eco-options may reduce their overall carbon footprints. But the carbon savings from the use of those acquisitions will be outweighed by commercial neglect of all the others consumers (including the 80 percent in the OECD) whose basic social needs are still unmet. The immediate upshot for the eco-haves will be access to greened enclaves, or fortified resource islands, protected and cut off from the human and natural sacrifice zones on the other side of the proverbial tracks.

The enclave scenario is already visible in most of our large cities, where the creditors (in the reversed terms of carbon debt) have been marooned in center cities or inner suburban rings, or, increasingly, are now stranded in the foreclosure belts of the urban fringe where they had to "drive to qualify" for subprime mortgages. Isolated from amenities, living-wage jobs, and nutritious food, and exposed to the legacy of toxic waste sites and hazardous industry, they are casualties of decades of urban policies tilted sharply toward the needs of more affluent eco debtors. The disparity between their substandard urban ecology and the fortified environments of elites is even sharper in the case of the undocumented immigrant service class. Detained and deported even when they are being sought out for use as a cheap and disposable workforce, a great number of today's transnational migrants are actually climate refugees, and are therefore creditors in their own right. What are they owed and how should those obligations be discharged?

DEBTS TO THE DISPLACED

The plight of environmental migrants, forced off their land and deprived of their livelihoods by climate change, is another component of ecological debt that was highlighted at Cochabamba precisely because it had received scant attention at the Copenhagen meetings. Environmental refugees are the most tangible human evidence of climate change impacts. Their numbers were in the tens of millions globally by 2000, and estimates from the IPCC, the 2006 Stern Report, and other sources predict that climate change will generate from two hundred million to as many as one billion migrants by 2050.[7] To date, no international convention has recognized the needs and rights of climate migrants, even though the Red Cross estimated that, by 2010, they had outnumbered the population of refugees from war and violence.[8] Nor is it clear that standard legal recognition would necessarily address their predicament—it may simply create yet another level of second class immigrant status for migrants to be held in the limbo of refugee camps and detention centers, or lost in the maze of temporary visa categories.

Yet these migrants are living embodiments of the dilemmas created by climate debt. Most of them arrive in a semi-indentured state, bound by personal debts generated by transit and recruitment fees. Yet even before they lift a finger to perform vital services, the host populace, in its capacity as climate debtor, is already beholden to them. What rights or resources should migrants expect as redress from hosts whose high-carbon lifestyle is responsible for displacing them from their lands and livelihoods? Surely they are owed sanctuary and civil protection at the very least, but other forms of restitution may well be brought to the table on their behalf in the years to come.

The longstanding religious right of sanctuary was revived by U.S. churches in the 1980s and extended to refugees from Ronald Reagan's wars in Central America. When the New Sanctuary Movement sprang up in the 2000s to provide asylum to immigrants facing deportation, the backlash was fomented at the state level. Arizona's notorious 2010 anti-immigrant law, SB 1070, made a point of banning sanctuary cities in the state, and spawned a wave of copycat legislation in others. Instead of forbidding city employees and police officers from asking people about their immigration status, as had been the rule in sanctuary cities, SB 1070 explicitly enjoined them to do so. From the perspective of climate justice, it was notable that Arizona emerged as the ground zero for nativist sentiment. After all, much of the state is in the bull's eye of climate change, heating up and drying out faster than any other region in the Northern hemisphere. Of course, the warming does not stop at the border. The impact on soil erosion in Northern Mexico from the decline in precipitation has also been significant, and studies predict that rainfall in those regions could decrease by 70 percent by the century's end. A significant portion of the Mexican border-crossers to Arizona have been displaced from their land and livelihoods, and should be classed as climate migrants.[9] Their Anglo tormentors in Sheriff Joe Arpaio's Maricopa County are also their climate debtors, because the carbon emissions pumped into the air above metro Phoenix are responsible, however indirectly, for setting these migrants in motion. In time, these migrants and their children may have their own carbon-conscious version of the retort offered by post-colonials when they settled in cities like London and Paris: "we are here because you were there."

The bitter fight over immigration in the militarized U.S borderlands is a harbinger of the "climate wars" to come, when the threat of global warming will be used to shape immigration policies around a *de facto* program for conserving rich nations and regions as eco-havens. In the rapidly greening enclaves of North America and Fortress Europe, the prevailing mentality is hostile to the idea of offering safe harbor to outsiders. Perhaps these enclaves are the modern equivalent of treasure hoards, which were wealth deposits hidden or stockpiled in moments of danger, to be retrieved later when needed by surviving elites. Aside from monetary fortune, today's hoards encompass a variety of physical assets, energy and communication infrastructure, and technical know-how, but they also include contractual claims, through financial debt, on future wages. Bespoke services, offering private firefighters, police, medical, and engineering personnel, are already available to elites who are all but building their own survival arks in high-security, enclaved real estate, often in several different countries to ensure the best escape location.

The resource enclave is the restrictive model for border politics in Northern countries, but its exclusionist spirit can also be detected *within* these borders in the patterns of eco-apartheid that exhibit stark divisions across metro regions. Climate-induced disasters on the scale of Hurricane Katrina and super-storm

Sandy readily expose the uneven impacts within cities, disproportionately affecting populations with the least resources, while others stay high and dry. Indeed, each of these disasters generated its own climate migrants: thousands displaced from their homes and communities, not just on a short-term basis, but permanently. Those with personal transport were able to escape the brunt of the hurricanes' impacts. Residents who had no way of getting out were trapped in devastated and dangerous neighborhoods with no power or food. Prisoners of their own houses and apartments, they were bereft of state emergency relief. Before the story moved on, twenty-four-hour media scrutiny brought their plight to global public attention.

Waterfront Devastation from Hurricane Sandy, November 2012 (courtesy MTL)

Hurricane Sandy also left a trail of devastation and a large death toll in Haiti, Cuba, the Bahamas, Jamaica, and Puerto Rico—in Haiti alone, Sandy destroyed 70 percent of the crops. But the world pays much more attention to a spectacular disaster in a rich city, especially one like New York, where the floodwaters inundated parts of the Financial District. The story met all the requirements of a Hollywood eco-apocalypse (New York City has been inundated many times on film) brought on suddenly and violently by an unanticipated climate trigger, as in Roland Emmerich's *The Day After Tomorrow* (2004). The much slower declines of our daily eco-apocalypse do not make headlines, let alone scripts for epic disaster movies. Yet documented consequences of anthropogenic global warming already include the steady retreat of glaciers, tundra permafrost, and sea ice; ocean acidification, salinization of soil and desertification; habitat degradation, land inundation, mega-droughts, loss of food security, and mass species extinctions, in addition to the damage from the more frequent occurrences of extreme-weather events. All the available evidence shows that these impacts have been occurring for some time, and that some are proceeding much more rapidly than predicted. But the declines are still not abrupt enough to register as catastrophic in the popular imagination.[10]

A similar predicament applies to climate migrants themselves. They are only noticed when they are in motion, and they only generate news and opinion when they cross borders into rich countries. China, for example, has millions of internal climate migrants—displaced by increased droughts, flooding, coastal erosion, saltwater inundation, glacial melt in the Himalayas, and shifting agricultural zones—but they are not identified as such, or counted as a population distinct from economic migrants. So, too, climate change affects people all over the world who cannot move for one reason or another, but this population is not recognized or enumerated as climate victims. They are only counted if and when they are displaced and become visible refugees, because a population in motion is perceived as a social or political, or at best, humanitarian, problem. Other forms of institutional authority identify them directly as threats. In 2010, for the first time, the Pentagon's Quadrennial Defense Review included climate change in its assessment of strategic threats.[11] But as early as 2003, a Department of Defense study explicitly warned: "climate change could become such a challenge that mass emigration results as the desperate peoples seek better lives in regions such as the United States that have the resources to adapt."[12]

Disasters that displace people *en masse* often give rise to our most noble expressions of common humanity. Rebecca Solnit's book *A Paradise Built in Hell* offers many case-studies of extraordinary altruism in the wake of catastrophes. Affected communities resort to social cooperation more readily than to regressive, anti-social behavior. "Horrible in itself," she writes, "disaster is sometimes a back door into paradise, the realm in which we are who we hope to be, to do the work we desire, and each are our sister's and brother's keeper."[13] These reserves of fraternal care underpin the kind of self-organization that anarchists like Solnit would like to bring into being. In rebuilding their distressed communities, usually with the help of outsiders, survivors learn and earn solidarity; they forge new kinds of fellow-feeling with their neighbors and their former adversaries, and strengthen what may previously have been a shallow network of informal ties and acquaintances. The trauma of common adversity, in other words, can help to originate new regenerative pathways of social life.

There were many stories like this about Katrina and Sandy, and they extended to the relief workers, especially in the extensive Occupy Sandy operation, which offered many of the volunteers a second chance to create the culture of mutual aid that Zuccotti Park hosted before the evictions of November 2011. In addition to reaching populations far beyond the orbit of the Occupy core, Occupy Sandy proved more effective and efficient than anything the state agencies like FEMA or the major aid NGOs like the Red Cross could muster. That forms of spontaneous self-organization proved superior to the mobilization of the state was held up as proof of anarchist concepts, but there were other forces with their eye on Sandy's aftermath, and they were not so benign.

The pattern of disaster capitalism, analyzed so well by Naomi Klein, explains how a distressed community with its defenses down becomes easy prey for profiteers of every stripe.[14] Even worse, a disaster or manufactured crisis is seized upon as an opportunity to restructure the local economy to the advantage of a small number of powerful, interested parties. For example, in the weeks after Sandy made landfall, banks were circling around its victims, offering special recovery loans for those who had maxed out on FEMA loans—the primary form of government relief on offer. One such loan pitch from JPMorgan Chase came carefully wrapped in phony compassion:

> "We have empowered our employees to be very accommodating to your hurricane-related circumstances in waiving fees, including the early withdrawal fees on most CDs to help customers with their financial situation ... We are a national bank, but the Tri-State area is home to many of us, too. We know we can't replace what people may have lost, but we will do what we can to help make the rebuilding easier."

Both government and private sector responses came in the form of personal loans, pushing the distressed into a new kind of debt

Occupy Sandy and Rolling Jubilee—Disaster and Debt (courtesy Strike Debt)

trap where their ability to recover from the storm meant taking on a long-term financial burden. *Shouldering the Costs*, a Strike Debt report based on field observations and community forums, showed that many of those taking out disaster loans were already stressed by lost equity from the housing crash. With no other credible options, they were being set up to deliver a new round of money transfers to the financial services industry. As to who should have been shouldering the costs, the report fingered several big players in the FIRE and energy industries:

> "Will [these costs] be borne by a billionaire mayor and his close friends in the real estate industry who rezoned and developed the coastline at an unprecedented pace, even as the Army Corps of Engineers ranked New York at the top of the list of cities most vulnerable to a storm surge? Will the federal government that refused to make the necessary infrastructure investments to protect us pick up the tab? Will the private insurers who accepted premiums year after year step up to pay for the damage they led us to believe they would cover? Or will those costs be borne by the fossil fuel companies and their lobbyists who have done everything in their power to make sure that radical changes to our atmosphere continue at a rapid pace, making all of us more vulnerable to natural disaster?[15]"

For the time being, it was clear that those footing the bill would be the individuals in the path of the storm, and that lenders would be profiting royally from the outcome. As for the economic reconstruction to follow, studies of rehabilitation after Katrina and 9/11 show a vigorous pattern of upward wealth redistribution. Market-centered policies focusing on tax breaks and private sector subsidies were favored over direct government outlays, and so developers prospered at the expense of the public benefit.[16] In the wake of Katrina, low-income populations were discouraged from returning to their communities, damaged public schools were closed and replaced with privatized alternatives, community-oriented hospitals were also replaced with higher-end private facilities, and devastated residential neighborhoods were turned over to large developers.[17] After 9/11, the biggest beneficiaries of the Liberty Bonds issued to assist in reconstruction were Larry Silverstein, owner of the World Trade Center site, Goldman Sachs, and the Bank of America. These bonds and other subsidies stimulated investment in Lower Manhattan's high-end real estate market, but did little to provide livelihoods to underemployed low-income residents of adjacent neighborhoods like Chinatown and the Lower East Side.

Mayor Bloomberg's appointment of Marc Ricks, a vice-president at Goldman Sachs, to the business-dominated team overseeing the Hurricane Sandy recovery efforts was an early indication that the crisis might be used to promote deregulation, reduce public services, and reward entrepreneurial business development. The ensuing face-off about the future of the city's waterfront offered stark choices. Should residents retreat altogether from the hundred-year flood zone A in the face of near-certain inundation, or should developers be greenlighted to build fortified enclaves capable of withstanding storm surges and tidal encroachment? Much of the city's public housing is situated in evacuation zones A or B, and so either option will once again entail the involuntary displacement of populations that were pushed out of more central locations by urban renewal programs in the 1960s and 1970s.[18] In the last two decades, New York's waterfront was increasingly targeted for upmarket development, and so its communities have been in transition from low-income to high-income. The latter fared a lot better during Sandy, bolstering the developers' argument for fortification. But the asset valued most by developers—the rising commodity price of waterfront land—is now in direct conflict with the social character of zone A land to act as an absorbent buffer of water from storm surges, as wetlands have traditionally done.

Mayor Bloomberg's support for the developers' claim was unequivocal: "We cannot and will not abandon our waterfront," he declared, announcing his administration's plan to follow the traditional strategy of the Army Corps of Engineers for shoring up by using protective bulwarks like flood walls, breakwaters, levees, sand dunes, and double-dunes.[19] It remains to be seen whether his successor will follow through on this plan. The Corps' model of beach and wall restoration, leaning heavily on federal funding and associated more and more in the public mind with the protection of privileged beachfront homeowners, has come under harsh scrutiny. Whatever the outcome, the future of zone A is not just a choice about how to respond to rising seas (a debate that is relevant to vulnerable coastal communities all over the world). The decision to develop or retreat will also reflect how longstanding patterns of environmental injustice continue to play out in different parts of the same city.

Environmental justice, roughly summarized, is aimed at combating the uneven distribution of resources, amenities and hazards across an entire metro area. Probably the starkest indicator is the disparity in life expectancy between residents in neighborhoods at either end of the socioeconomic scale. In Washington DC, there is a seven year difference, Kansas City shows a fifteen year spread, and in New Orleans, the gap in life expectancy between neighborhoods is as great as twenty-five years.[20] In self-assessing their performance, urban managers who want to gloss over this highly uneven pattern prefer to record their success at reducing the overall carbon footprint of their cities. The sustainable cities movement has generally encouraged this mentality. Taking an entire city's carbon budget as the unit of political performance allows officials to turn a blind eye to metropolitan-scale inequalities, and also to the existence of local climate debts. In this respect, it is worth noting that international climate justice was modeled on the environmental justice movement that emerged within American cities during the 1980s to combat the unequal siting of hazardous industry and toxic waste. Indeed, the Bali Principles of Climate Justice, adopted in 2002, were based on the Environmental Justice Principles blueprint, developed at the 1991 People of Color Environmental Justice Leadership Summit in Washington.

Hurricane Sandy had a rude impact on how we think about urban sustainability. For some, the storm's urgent showcasing of climate-driven damage suggested that the window for sustainability is over. They have concluded, and not unreasonably, that there is insufficient political will to avert drastic climate change by reducing emissions. Instead, they have more fully embraced the mindset of adaptive resilience—a survivor's mentality. Adaptive resilience is all about weathering the worst assaults, in the case of storms, through building hard-walled fortifications, or "softer" shorelines edges. Focusing on the immediate physical defense of communities inevitably invites us to think of them more as exclusion zones than, say, as safe harbors for climate migrants. Prioritizing this view feeds into the "lifeboat ethic" scenario popularized by Garret Hardin in the 1970s, which tried to rationalize how, in a world of limited or diminishing resources, the affluent in the North could ill-afford to take on board the world's impoverished peoples. Giving priority to the protection of resource islands is a far cry from the course of action that rich cities could follow if they really were responding to the challenge of climate justice. They could cut emissions, for example, to allow less affluent cities to use their carbon allotment to develop out of poverty, or they could levy carbon taxes to pay for the humane resettlement of climate migrants.

Up until now, climate justice claims have been made through the nation-state architecture of the UNFCCC treaty-making process. But this framework for distributive justice has proven to be frustrating at best. Could cities do better? More progress in climate policymaking has been made at the urban level than at the state or national level.[21] One of the reasons for this is that City Hall does not usually make policy about energy generation and therefore is not subject to fierce lobbying from the fossil fuel industry. Urban politicians may have little sway over the biggest polluters, but they have made greater strides than their federal counterparts in energy conservation, emission mitigation, and zero-carbon alternatives in transportation and consumption. Can they help cities lead the way in recognizing and repaying climate debts to urban creditors in the South? If not, how can non-state actors and communities self-organize with those goals in mind, given that urban managers tend to neglect social divisions within their own bailiwick, responding best to the interests of the well-heeled?

DELIVERY OPTIONS

In 2010, Bolivia introduced an UNFCCC proposal, based on the Cochabamba agreements, which defines climate debt as comprising two portions: an "emissions debt" and an "adaptation debt." The emissions portion is based on the denial to developing countries of "their fair share of atmospheric space." Under this rubric, sharp reductions in the domestic emissions of energy-intensive countries are required in order to free up space for others to develop their way out of poverty. Any over-consumption of their carbon allocation would require these countries to pay the emissions debt. The goal here would be to "decolonize the atmosphere," by ensuring that poor countries do not to have to forego development opportunities in the interest of containing global emissions. The adaptation portion of climate debt is based on culpability for damage already done. Repayment would require the beneficiaries of industrialization that caused climate change to compensate the victims of its impacts. This remittance would cover not only reparations for the damage but also the costs of absorbing and combating impacts in the future. Financing the application of clean energy technologies (and renouncing the associated intellectual property rights) would be a large part of these adaptation costs.

To respond adequately to both portions, the historical carbon powers would have to acknowledge that their climate debts are obligations. To date, the preferred response of high carbon emitters like the U.S. is to offer "climate aid" as a discretionary act, and effectively as a one-time payoff. Indeed, within the UNFCCC process, "climate finance" has emerged as the term of choice. In Copenhagen, rich countries promised $30 billion in climate financing as part of a fast-track aid package for the first three years, with pledges at a higher level after 2012. At the end of the fast-track period, the U.S. reported $7.5 billion in contributions, though most of it had been accounted for through mitigation in the form of domestic emission cuts. These reductions, moreover, were achieved largely through the risk-intensive extraction of natural gas by hydrofracking, and also as a result of the industrial slowdown from the Great Recession. A much smaller allocation (less than 20 percent by some estimates) had been budgeted as adaptation costs.[22] Overall, only 12 percent of the climate funding from the top contributors went to adaptation.[23] In the meantime, critics contend that much of this assistance would have been offered anyway under the rubric of "foreign aid," or that it has been diverted from other forms of development goals in spite of the UNFCCC requirement that climate funding be "new and additional." The multilateral Green Climate Fund, conceived at the Cancun meetings in 2010, has yet to open for business. Delayed by the footdragging of high emitters, especially the U.S., Saudi Arabia, and Australia, even the fund's advocates have low expectations of meeting its goal of $100 billion annually in pledges.

At the most recent UNFCCC meetings in Doha, a fragile alliance between the EU, the Alliance of Small Island States, and the Least Developed Countries pushed the debt claims further. Despite initial resistance from the U.S. negotiators, the responsibility to mitigate "loss and damage from climate change" was incorporated into the international legal record for the first time, but there was no agreement on a monetary target or a time line for climate finance. In addition, the U.S. negotiators strongly opposed any mention of "compensation" in the final Doha drafts, or indeed any language that implied legal liability for repayment of a climate debt, however it may be calculated. Avoiding any implication of blame, this allowed any payments to continue to register as "aid," disbursed (it remains to be decided by which mechanism) as an act of benevolence and not as part of a statutory obligation.

For many of its critics, the greatest shortcoming of the UNFCCC process of international allocations is that it does not account for differential rights and responsibilities within the borders of Southern nations. Rising emissions and historical accumulation on the part of homegrown elites are contributing factors to maldistribution of carbon benefits within those borders. "Who owes who?" is a question that must also be answered on a local basis, because each country has its own "odious" climate debtors, whether they are local allies of multinational plunder, or profiteers in their own right from the extractive industries that lie at the heart of the climate crisis. There is no doubt that some of the culpability for the outsourcing of dirty industries (remember Larry Summers' infamous 1991 World Bank memo: "the economic logic behind dumping a load of toxic waste on the lowest-wage country is impeccable ... under-populated countries in Africa are vastly under-polluted") must be laid at the door of local officials or capitalists who gained at the cost of their compatriots.

These are the same groups who lobby lawmakers in developing countries for headlong development of extractive industries—oil, gas, coal, copper, iron ore, lithium, and other mineral mining. The industrial policy of extractivism runs directly counter to the indigenous Andean philosophies underlying the Cochabamba ethos of protecting the rights of nature and Pachamama (Mother Earth). Latin American leftist governments justify their export programs based on large-scale extractivism when the proceeds are used to fund social programs, effectively passing on a large share of the earnings to the mass of the population. Yet the expansion of such industrial activities has only dismayed those who hoped that the left turn in the region would deliver alternative development pathways, distinct from the colonial patterns of resource expropriation.[24] Many of the extractors are state-owned, but a good number are privately run by families with a long history of wealth and power in the region. While their enduring economic and political influence is dwarfed by that wielded in North America by the likes of the Koch brothers, it is still a significant factor in the makeup of climate justice, and needs to be accounted for in any repayment program that takes redistribution as a ranking principle. How can the UNFCCC's international carbon allocation system incorporate these local debts? Can it guarantee that climate debt payments, if and when they are made, will not unduly benefit the elites of the creditor countries? How much of the compensation will get to those who need it most?

Similar questions are often asked of development aid programs. Economists have shown that such aid tends to widen income gaps in receiving countries as a result of corruption and graft by government officials and their cronies. Others point to the dodgy behavior of donors; foreign aid is rarely altruistic, since it is usually dictated by geopolitical strategy or by the commercial interests of donor countries and institutions. Inevitably, this strain of aid-bashing will apply to any system of climate finance unless there is transparent tracking of the funding to ensure it is flowing through the most effective channels and not into the kleptocracy. One way to circumvent these pitfalls would be to make payments in the form of a basic income to all residents. This income, unconditionally allocated and not subject to means-testing, would provide a green dividend to low-income households and communities that fall outside of the typical disbursement orbit of foreign aid funds. Infrastructural sustainability is beyond their economic reach, but a minimum income, if it was packaged as a common ecological premium—a fruit of the earth, to be shared with respect to Mother Earth—would be accordant with the spirit of *buen vivir,* or good holistic living (as opposed to the materialist "good life") that was championed at Cochabamba, and adopted thereafter as a guiding philosophy of the climate justice movement.

The achievement of an independent income for women would reduce some of the risks endemic to a gendered division of labor. So, too, basic income would be a debt-free alternative to the kind of high-interest micro-financing that is increasingly predatory in practice, as more large financial institutions move into the poverty business. Indeed, a pilot program for basic income in Otjivero, Namibia demonstrated a number of positive ripple effects, increasing the community's overall income to a level well above the aggregate amount of the grant that funded the program. Poverty, household debt, and child malnutrition rates fell, and economic activity shot up.[25]

Payment of climate debts through basic income could be funded most easily by a universal carbon tax, with the additional advantage that such a tax would penalize high carbon users in the South. Another source could be a tax on financial transactions akin to the Tobin tax most recently proposed by the European Commission. After all, the original motivation of the climate justice movement was to seek cancellation of the financial debts of Southern eco creditors. If financial creditors refuse to go along with this compact (even when asked to do so by the Paris Club or London Club), then a portion of their profits should simply be absorbed and redirected though this Robin Hood form of taxation. The third provider of funding must be the fossil fuel industries themselves. Their lavish profits depend on their immunity from paying the costs of pollution and ecological damage from the origination and use of their products. Taxing extraction and processing at the point of production and in the name of climate justice would address a longstanding complaint that such costs are unfairly externalized, to be borne solely by users or taxpayers. Alaska's popular program of an annual disbursement to all residents from oil revenue (the Permanent Fund Dividend) is a model that could be reframed to reflect the spirit of climate justice. Bringing the basic income into being is a long-term project—the political work would require heavy lifting in both the North and the South—but it stands out as one viable model for minimizing the pitfalls and maximizing the merits involved in repaying a debt that really should be honored.

In the North, the provision of basic income, derived from the three funding sources cited above, could also be used to promote environmental justice at home. The international face of the climate crisis may well be the tragic spectacle of tropical islands disappearing beneath rising seas, but climate change is also a poisonous reality at the point of industrial production. In the U.S., for example, think of the communities exposed to toxins from the pollution of coal-fired power stations or ash from the blasting for mountain top removal, not to mention the cancerous impact of uranium mining on Indian reservations.

Since basic income is, by definition, divorced from labor, it would be a start in weaning us off the habitual toil expected in a compulsory work society. So, too, it could help to ease the "just transition" of labor away from high-carbon livelihoods. Labor advocates in the North have not found it easy to make connections to a climate justice movement dominated by indigenous rights and the cause of sufficiency agriculture. Urban workers in fully industrialized societies find it hard to identify with the Cochabamba credo of *buen vivir.* After all, the labor movement in the global North has long been hitched to the consumerist wagon of the "good life" principle that stands in diametrical opposition to *buen vivir* because it is associated, in the Cochabamba mind, with plunder and unfettered materialist growth. While they may share the same enemies, enriched and empowered by thirty years of neoliberalism, the interests and priorities of such workers are not the same as those of dispossessed *campesinos* and rainforest communities.

Where, in the North, do we find most evidence of Cochabamba's agrarianist consciousness? Aside from indigenous activists, the new generation farmers of the food movement would be the most closely aligned. Their zeal for local control, healthy provision, food security, and self-organization has been surprisingly contagious. Shrinking cities like Detroit and Baltimore are emerging as centers of food justice, through grassroots urban farming, with the potential to build alternative economies in the hollowed-out core of the old. For ex-industrial workers, abandoned in the "food deserts" of these inner cities, the chance to reinvent livelihoods literally in their own backyards is a significant exercise of social and environmental justice. In more traditional agricultural locations, however, the movement has its own labor problems, since food activists routinely ignore the dependence of their idealized small growers on underpaid and marginalized migrant workers.[26]

With the prospect of lowered emissions on the table, an overriding concern for labor is that well-paying jobs (in the heavily unionized dirty energy sector) will be lost in the shift to clean-tech industries. The International Trade Union Confederation

(ITUC) lobbied hard for the inclusion of "just transition" in the initial drafts of the Copenhagen Accord, but it was dropped from the final wording, only to be incorporated two years later in the voluntary "shared vision" adopted at the Cancun summit in December 2010. The Cancun signatories pledged to "promote a just transition of the workforce, the creation of decent work and quality jobs in accordance with nationally defined development priorities and strategies and contributing to building new capacity for both production and service-related jobs in all sectors, promoting economic growth and sustainable development." Looking to embed the rights of workers displaced or sidelined by the conversion to a low-carbon future, the ITUC also pushed for basic International Labour Organization rights regarding workplace democracy. Given the long-term prospect of mass joblessness and deepening precarity, a just transition would more fairly distribute the costs and benefits of low-carbon policies, especially when guided by the principles of climate justice.

Particularly important, in this regard, is the need to counter efforts on the part of big polluters to divert accountability for direct climate debt repayment by passing on the costs to individuals. A good example of this neoliberal tendency is the growing habit of assessing the carbon footprint of every product and every personal action. Quantifying the world's energy throughput on the micro-level of personal conduct is becoming a pseudo political obsession. In some ways, it is a perverse spin on the statistical tyranny of the GDP, reducing our actions and our use of material things to a dull data set—the outcome being a moral assessment of our individual thermodynamic performance. Carbon-Neutral Man is the prescribed goal, a model of ascetic behavior that is the exact obverse of the wasteful hyperconsumer. Transferring the burden of compliance onto the conscience of individuals in this way absolves the polluters who have the largest responsibility to repay climate debts and who can most effectively reduce emissions. As with most expressions of debt-based morality, we must reject this tendency, or turn it back onto the profiteers. Hydrocarbon should be an outlawed byproduct of our civilization, not its loud scourge.

DISSOLVING THE MARRIAGE OF DEBT AND GROWTH

In the aftermath of the 2008 crash, the financial engineering of Wall Street was subject to sweeping censure, and some regulatory bills—though destined to be gutted or diluted—were pushed into the legislative hopper. Seldom was there a better time for the advocates of alternatives to the debt-money system to get a fair hearing. Yet the recession bit so deep, decimating the workforce in so many countries, that policy efforts to jumpstart economic recovery were almost all aimed at regenerating consumption growth along lines that required the resumption of debt-financing. Restoring a positive GDP track was the ubiquitous goal, whether in the initial neo-Keynesian phase of public money stimulus—targeted at green job creation in sustainable industries—or in the subsequent round of austerity policies aimed at cutting public expenditures to the bone. For too many of the world's economic managers, the favored recovery vehicle was the one that promised the fastest return to business as usual, in the form of debt-driven expansion of production and consumption. Never mind that this model is ecologically unsustainable and economically calamitous. The gospel of growth is so universally accepted that it is considered heretical, in almost all institutional quarters, to think that a zero-growth economy, or one governed by de-growth policies, could generate respectable employment and income levels, let alone deliver prosperity.

Tim Jackson, Economics Commissioner on the U.K. Sustainable Development Commission, has neatly summarized both sides of what he calls "the dilemma of growth." On the one hand, "growth is unsustainable—at least in its current form. Burgeoning resource consumption and rising environmental costs are compounding profound disparities in social well-being." On the other hand, "'de-growth' is unstable—at least under present conditions. Declining consumer demand leads to rising unemployment, falling competitiveness and a spiral of recession." Solutions to this very real dilemma are desperately needed. Given how little the banks have mended their lawless conduct, another crash and an even deeper recession are likely prospects in the near future. The conventional response, proposed by advocates of light-green capitalism, is "decoupling," which calls for continued economic growth while relying on capitalist efficiencies to reduce the impacts on natural resources relative to the GDP. Jackson himself rejects this "relative decoupling" ("doing more with less") because any savings will almost always be cancelled by the corresponding growth in consumption. His preferred path is "absolute decoupling," because reducing resource impacts in absolute terms is the only plausible way of remaining within ecological limits. In his judgment, "simplistic assumptions that capitalism's propensity for efficiency will allow us to stabilize the climate and protect against resource scarcity are nothing short of delusional."[1]

Rethinking prosperity in nonmaterialistic ways, as recommended by Jackson (and his collaborators on the Redefining Prosperity project), is crucial to changing consciousness and, ultimately, policy. [2] Accounting for people's real needs—to live in a just society, to act as free persons, to access common cultural goods, to enjoy gratifying labor, and to feel connected to nonhuman nature—is surely the key to establishing more useful indexes of well-being than the GDP metric currently offers. But toppling GDP from its throne will also mean confronting the power of the financial industries to dictate common sense notions of prosperity, while building an alternative economy that is not driven by their predatory debt system.

After five years of recessionary stagnation, the pressure to increase GDP growth rates is all-consuming, and, for the past several decades, expansion of credit has been the preferred, all-purpose, monetary instrument for the job. In the most recent version of this model, central banks like the Federal Reserve and the Bank of England have maintained rock-bottom interest rates and printed mountains of money, through quantitative easing, in order to help the economy "grow its way" out of the recession. An estimated $2.3 trillion has been printed in the U.S. and

$545 billion in the U.K., much of it ending up in the accounts of banks that continue to resist lending to small businesses in the real economy. Although dirt-cheap money has been made readily available to large corporations and banks, they won't invest it in the absence of a speculative bubble, so they are sitting on vast amounts of cash, much of it parked offshore in tax havens. Even during a boom, rent-seeking money does not circulate in a way that stimulates conventional growth in the real economy, but in times like these, with austerity and debt deflation in the saddle, it resembles an idle surplus that begs to be invested in productive channels.

The economic managers who introduced austerity policies often cited the controversial 2010 Reinhart-Rogoff thesis that national growth will decline by 2 percent when external debt reaches 60 percent of GDP, and then fall off by 50 percent when the debt level reaches 90 percent. The thesis was fully discredited, in the spring of 2013, for its flawed methodology and inaccurate supporting data. But the connection Reinhart and Rogoff drew between debt and growth had a powerful residual appeal, and with good reason, because it was the legacy of several decades of hardwired assumptions about their mutual interdependence. Hence the continued reliance on policies aimed at restoring the *status quo ante*—the era when national growth machines were fueled by easy borrowing and when the expectation of high GDP growth reassured creditors of lucrative returns. From the onset of the Bretton Woods system, this was the sanguine, and relatively stable, formula to which the managers of national economies in the global North pledged their allegiance.

For sure, there were periodic crashes, occasioned by new heights of speculative activity. But the anchoring mechanism of growth recovery in each case was the expansion of credit, eased by financial deregulation, that made it possible to wheel and deal with an ever greater variety of credit forms within the banking sector. The severity of the post-2008 recession has called into question aspects of this debt-growth system. Long-term stagnation, with only minimal growth, is a distinct possibility,[3] and some national leaders, like Nicolas Sarkozy, have flirted with the idea of replacing GDP with an index of well-being that measures factors other than productivity or income. Although it will take more than a new yardstick of happiness to forge an alternative pathway, one thing is certain. A successor economy will not rely on GDP-indexed growth, nor can it. The cost—in carbon and other resources—is already far in excess of planetary limits. But to learn how to live outside of the fatal axis that links predatory debt and unsustainable growth, we have to first understand how they came to be mutually dependent.

BIGGERING AND BEGGARING

Consider the passage in Dr. Seuss's *The Lorax* where the Once-ler describes the growth of his ruinous operations:

"I meant no harm. I most truly did not. But I had to grow bigger. So bigger I got. I biggered my factory. I biggered my roads. I biggered my wagons. I biggered the loads ... And I biggered my money, which everyone needs."

This is not a bad summary of the mentality of business growth for a producer, right down to the self-serving belief that he "meant no harm." As for the money that "everyone needs," in the Once-ler's case, this would be the capital he requires for expansion—and he makes it quite clear that he has no choice but to expand. In the case of his customers, the money is what they need to go on consuming his products. Would the Once-ler put it differently if he were in the business of finance? If he had shareholders to satisfy, then the responsibility to generate returns for them would require him to grow the enterprise. If he were selling credit and other debt products, the loans he made would register as assets—a form of growth in their own right. He would also need clients with the expectation, at least, of more money, from growth, in their futures. Without that assurance, he would not be able to extend the loans, let alone hope for a tidy profit from them. The Once-ler was ruined when he exhausted the raw materials (truffala trees) for his products (thneeds), and *The Lorax* does a good job of depicting this. If he were a banker, his continued ability to make money from money alone would depend on an expanding economy, or else on high-risk gambling. It would only be exhausted if future growth contracted to zero and there was no available income left to repay his loans.

Borrowers will have more money in the future to pay back loans only if there is a likelihood of economic growth, and so growth is what allows bankers to lend money into existence. It is important to grasp that they do not possess the money hitherto. Fatally, the public imagination retains the image of a lender retrieving a bag of money from the vault to bestow it on a credit-worthy borrower. This imagined scenario accounts, in large part, for the guilt we experience if we can't repay what we imagine to be the bank's own cash. Bankers have no reason to dispel that self-serving image, but it is quite illusory; in most instances, the banks are creating money *ex nihilo*. The system of fractional reserve banking allows them to make loans far in excess of the reserves they hold in the form of customers' deposits—in the U.S., ten dollars of loans for every one on reserve—while the use of derivatives allows them even higher leverage ratios. The money, which is created specifically as interest-bearing debt, springs to life only at the moment that a borrower signs a loan agreement and promises to pay back even more of it to the bank. That promise is only credible in the context of general growth, which is why growth is so key to the business of lending.

In most cases, all that is required for the loan to exist is the addition of some numbers on a computer screen. Nor is the amount of the loan deducted from a bank's accounts, as one might debit some asset that is no longer in one's possession. On the contrary, the bank adds to its recorded assets the full amount to be paid back over the lifetime of the loan. So if my daughter borrows $50,000 to help pay for college tuition, the bank will effectively have created, say, $70,000 for itself (the estimated full amount, with interest, that the loan will return) which did not previously exist. This kind of phantom asset growth, none of which is actually earned, appears as if from nowhere, and it induces the more elaborate fantasy that, through the magic of compound interest (which Einstein pointedly described as "the eighth wonder of the world"), fictitious capital could expand the economy in a more or less limitless way. Wealth is thereby conjured, and in a way that completely circumvents the labor theory of value. When debt can apparently be created without much effort, it is no wonder that its value, as a percentage of GDP, can mushroom so quickly.

Few would conclude that this way of estimating worldly value, let alone well-being, is anything but irrational and illusory. But it does explain why creditors depend on growth forecasts to make paper claims on the future. Ideally, every percentage of GDP growth would equate, ultimately, to points on interest rates. However, since the interest rates are usually much higher than GDP growth rates, there is a chronic mismatch. This gap can be interpreted as evidence of the fundamental unsustainability of the debt-growth system, or its operationalization as a Ponzi scheme that can never pay for itself. According to the exponential growth rate of compound interest, debts will always multiply more rapidly than the ability to pay them. In theory, lending for profit shouldn't make sense unless borrowers have access to incomes that will grow at more or less the same rate as the interest. Anything less would make it difficult to collect the debt, which is why banks have invented all sorts of ways to pass on the risks through loan securitization, derivatives, and other forms of gambling. The ability to sell loans on the secondary market means that bankers do not have to care all that much in the short term whether or not the loans can be repaid. But their long-term business (do they ever think of that?) depends ultimately on an expanding surplus down the road or else debt service would cease. While a zero-growth economy might be an ecological necessity, it would be a banker's nightmare.

The GDP metric, which includes the valuation of transactions less fictitious than financial trades, is no less irrational as an index of social worth. GDP measures the total consumption of goods and services that are exchanged for money, and so it increases, for example, if you are in poor health and purchase medical services. If, on the other hand, you manage to keep yourself in good health through exercise or other homegrown preventive measures, you are doing nothing to help GDP. The same outcomes apply to almost anything you try to do by yourself. Purchasing a meal from a restaurant, as opposed to growing your own food and cooking it, is a boost for the GDP balance. Preserving part of a forest on your land as a form of natural capital or as a carbon sink won't show up, but selling the trees as timber commodities will. What this means is that people who are unhealthy, or who do not know how to cook, or who destroy natural resources are more or less ideal citizens in a capitalist growth economy, at least wherever GDP is accepted as an inventory of national well-being.

Needless to say, GDP is blind to the costs associated with environmental degradation, whether in the form of carbon emissions or through the exhaustion of natural resources. There are many other oversights. GDP neglects non-market activity such as the traditionally female sphere of unpaid household labor and child rearing; it overlooks gross economic inequality; and it cannot distinguish between useful expenditure on public infrastructure and wasteful spending on cleaning up after environmental disasters like oil spills or climate-driven hurricanes. Above all, in light of this book's topic, it does not account for the impact of indebtedness. It's all the same to GDP if I purchase a car because I got a raise, or if I acquired it through cranking up my credit card debt to untenable levels. As a result of stagnant or declining wages, an increasingly larger share of household consumption is debt-financed. No one should rationally view this debt-dependent consumption as a long-term component of well-being, and yet this is how it is recorded in a society that values growth above all other measures of progress, and makes the bulk of its consequential economic decisions on the basis of metrics like GDP.

Yet it is only quite recently that growth, as expressed by GDP, became the primary measure of a nation's aspirations. John Stuart Mill, the Victorian era's liberal apostle of progress, thought it reasonable, and indeed desirable, for human development to continue to flourish in a "stationary state of capital and wealth." Otherwise, he predicted that the environmental damage from economic and demographic growth would be too great, and "the earth must lose that great portion of its pleasantness which it owes to things that the unlimited increase of wealth and population would extirpate from it."[4] In the Marxist analytic tradition, growth was always seen as integral to any capitalist system of accumulation; capitalist enterprises must grow or die.

But it is only in the postwar years that GDP-indexed growth has come to be universally accepted as a society's principal standard of worth. In the course of that time span, the pursuit of growth has become a fetish, according to Clive Hamilton, assigned marvelous properties that are believed to irradiate society as a whole. Under such a belief system, a multitude of social ills are ameliorated, or cease to exist, when the all-purpose cure of growth is successfully applied.[5] Not surprisingly, four-fifths of U.S. growth has occurred in the last fifty years, much of it initially driven by Cold War competition to prove the superiority of a market economy.[6] Growth was an especially key component of the consensus mood that developed among business, political, and academic elites after 1945—it became a master-concept around which the interests of groups could be harmonized. In the immediate postwar years, for example, this growth consensus helped seal the social contract between state, capital, and labor. The underlying proposition was that growth, in the form of expanding production, emerging markets, and increased consumption, would generate benefits for all: political stability for governing elites, the consumer's good life for decently-paid workers, and respectable rates of profit for capital owners.

On the back of the expansionist boom, growthmanship spread abroad to close Western allies, like the U.K., and France, and established itself as the cardinal goal of statecraft for Cold War junior partners like Japan and West Germany—as well as for economies like South Korea and Taiwan "invited" to industrialize, and the broad spectrum of decolonizing countries eager to demonstrate they could thrive on their own. GDP growth was adopted as the preferred yardstick for national development, whether in the advanced or the developing world, and soon became a one-size-fits-all measure of how states were faring in their adaptation to the global capitalist economy. Falling growth rates, regarded as an early warning of a failing state, invited close scrutiny from the World Bank. For countries whose economies had been underdeveloped, taking on external loans to stimulate growth led them into the notorious debt trap, overseen and enforced by the International Monetary Fund. According to these norms, advocates of alternative forms of human development, especially those who favored more sustainable or "appropriate technologies," were simply treated as dropouts from modernity.

It was more difficult for elites to ignore *The Limits to Growth*, the momentous 1972 Club of Rome report which concluded that current rates of industrial growth could not be sustained ecologically in the long term. Based on computer modeling that simulated interactions between human systems and those of the Earth, the authors' predictions were based on extensive scientific evidence, and so their methodologies had to be vigorously challenged, as indeed they were, by technical experts. In the absence of any conclusive refutation, growth boosters proclaimed that technological innovations (usually ones that carry greater risks, such as fracking, tar-sands exploitation, and deep-water drilling) would enable physical limits on growth to be transcended. Over time, advocates of green capitalism learned how to better promote the energy efficiencies that could be achieved through adoption of their products. All the while, top-level economists, the high priests of growth, could be relied on to issue emphatic dismissals of any talk about limits. In 1993, Larry Summers, as chief economist of the World Bank, proclaimed that "there are no ... limits to the carrying capacity of the earth that are likely to bind at any time in the foreseeable future. There isn't a risk of an apocalypse due to global warming or anything else. The idea that we should put limits on growth because of some natural limit, is a profound error and one that, were it ever to prove influential, would have staggering social costs."[7] Anne Krueger, Summers' predecessor as World Bank chief economist, argued in 2003 that while economic growth generates an initial phase of ecological deterioration, increases in income allow countries to reduce pollution levels of their own accord, and "the turning point at which people begin choosing to invest in cleaning up and preventing pollution at a per capita GDP of about US $5,000."[8] No real evidence exists for such declarations. Economists like Summers and Krueger, who are consistently rewarded for their serviceability (until they become liabilities, as Summers did when he emerged as President Obama's ill-fated favorite to occupy the Federal Reserve chairmanship), are simply the court poets of our day, singing in the key of the royalists on top.

The *Limits to Growth* analysis was never seriously disputed. Most subsequent surveys, drawing on more advanced models, a wider range of experts, and updated scientific data, either reinforced or magnified the 1972 warning about the ruinous consequence of unrestrained growth. In reprisals of the initial study, twenty and thirty years later, the *Limits to Growth* team confirmed the original predictions that eco-collapse would result if current growth trends were to continue.[9] These reports were habitually disregarded by elites, and it is often concluded that they were brushed aside not because they convey an inconvenient truth but because the ideology of growth has attained a status akin to religious dogma. The same reasoning (or lack thereof) is often attributed to deniers of climate change. But another interpretation is that elites did heed the message of *The Limits to Growth*, and they responded by squirreling away whatever resources they could carry off from the commonweal.

Hoarding in anticipation of oncoming scarcity is a plausible explanation of the patterns of sharp upward wealth redistribution since the mid-1970s. The systematic capture of wealth and natural assets, whether in the form of income redistribution or land grabs (in the spirit of what David Harvey calls "accumulation by dispossession"), can be seen as a logical reaction to the evidence that absolute scarcity was on the horizon. This pattern of acquisitive conduct is evident in almost all developed or developing societies, but especially in the fast-growth economies whose Gini coefficients (the index of economic inequality in any society) enlarged significantly. Far from living in denial about the ecological costs of growth, beneficiaries of the finance-driven economy in particular have been behaving as if they know that the writing is on the wall—acting like secessionists from the 99 percent, building heavily fortified eco havens, seizing control of public assets through privatization, paying themselves ever larger bonuses and salaries, bribing politicians to pass creditor-friendly legislation, ransacking state resources to bail out their banks and mitigate the wreckage caused by their usurious lending practices, and militarizing police forces to protect their islands of privilege against dissenting debt peons.

This pillaging and hoarding has been aided and abetted by the gospel of growth, and its most effective technical amplifier has been the expansion and manipulation of household credit. After income faltered and stagnated, and goods production was internationalized, household debt became the only guarantor of consumption growth, and so it began its steady climb, delivering returns along the way to the creditor class. During the postwar boom decades that the French call "*les trentes glorieuses*," the gains from growth, primarily stimulated by government spending, had been more evenly shared. But the ability of the 1 percent to capture the lion's share of the proceeds from the late 1970s illustrates the central role of debt-financed consumer lending in channeling wealth upwards. Not only was credit the most efficient instrument of rent extraction and wealth redistribution, it was also adopted as the master-key to economic management and policy. The result was a comprehensive mode of governance—economic, social, and political—that positioned the creditor class beyond the reach of regulation, and capable of rebounding from its near self-destruction in 2008 by capturing almost all the gains in the zero-game scramble that followed.

In the wake of the 1970s slowdown, successive policy doctrines were aimed at reviving the steady growth rates of the post-war decades. The roll-call includes the supply-side monetarism of Reaganomics, which resulted in the United States moving from being the world's largest international creditor to the world's largest debtor nation; the successive waves of deregulation which permitted banks to "grow" the finance sector on the back of high-risk gambling; the upsurge of high-tech evangelism in the 1990s, which resulted in a massive equity crash from the overvaluation of the dotcom bubble; and the asset ownership creed of the 2000s, which brought a frenzy of personal debt leveraging to its catastrophic conclusion with the subprime mortgage crash. Each of these were efforts, fueled by the sharp expansion of credit, to chase up fake growth in the present through manipulating debt on the promise of growth in the future. One of the outcomes today is that financial services account for ever more accumulation (50 percent of non-farm business profits in the U.S.), though no one can say what social benefits they generate, or how they contribute to the well-being of society. Nor is the industry's share of GDP a certain thing, given how immaterial these services can be. Loans are recorded as purchased assets, but, just like that $70,000 booked by the issuer of my daughter's $50,000 student loan, they are quite fictitious; they don't exist in the present in any real way, and they are only realized if someone fully services the loan debt in the decades to come.

Given the bounty enjoyed by the kingpins of finance in the post-2008 years, they are not ready to acknowledge that the debt-growth system that served them so well for four decades may have reached its own limits. But steady accumulation from what Marx called "usury capital" depends, ultimately, on a supply of surplus income, and the surplus is dwindling fast. Put simply, there probably won't be sufficient income available in the future to pay back the loans. But when that happens, the creditor class will have no plan B to fall back on, except to pray for one last asset bubble, before the surplus is absorbed entirely, and the world's eco-systems enter a state of general collapse.

A NON-EXTRACTIVE CREDIT ECONOMY?

In previous chapters of this book, I have argued that debtors' resistance is only a prelude to the kind of just and sustainable society where socially productive credit would replace extractive lending as the backbone of the economy. At present, debt repudiation is the prerogative of the 1 percent. Bankers are the ones who expect to have their debts forgiven, and high-carbon industrialists, like the Koch brothers, are the ones who refuse to pay their own ecological debts. But the mantle of debt refusal is passing to those who have been asked to bear the largest burdens. When that happens, it should be in accord with ongoing efforts to build a new economy—based on mutual aid, common goods, social cooperation, and public affluence—and a real democracy—based on self-organization, full participation, and freedom from all kinds of coercion. Fledgling efforts are already underway, in a variety of forms, and so it may not require a herculean effort or state takeover to realize a post-capitalist system. In the section that follows, I offer a sampling of examples and trends, not a comprehensive survey (for that, see the Global Transition to a New Economy or the Intercontinental Network for the Promotion of Social Solidarity Economy—RIPESS).[10]

Some are demonstration projects, undertaken to show that it is possible to beat the debt predators. It was in this spirit, for example, that Strike Debt released the *Debt Resistors' Operations Manual* (DROM) in September 2012 (on the first anniversary of Occupy Wall Street) as a public education service—to provide practical advice to debtors about how to reduce, or free themselves from, their burdens. The DROM offers basic information, some of it culled from industry insiders, about the traps laid by lenders in each sector of debt—education, healthcare, housing, credit cards, fringe finance—and it informs readers about seeking active debt relief for themselves, through tactics ranging from renegotiation to outright evasion. While these are individual solutions, beneficial for debtors in a desperate situation, the DROM emphasizes throughout that the only effective way of combating the system is through collective action. Its presiding message is summarized thus:

> "To the financial establishment of the world, we have only one thing to say: We owe you nothing. To our friends, our families, our communities, to humanity and to the natural world that makes our lives possible, we owe you everything. Every dollar we take from a fraudulent subprime mortgage speculator, every dollar we withhold from the collection agency is a tiny piece of our own lives and freedom that we can give back to our communities, to those we love and we respect."

Taken as a general ethos, this version of Who Owes Who? suggests that the prevailing psychology of indebtedness needs to be turned upside down. As an economic precept, it points to ways in which a currently wasted surplus could be used to finance an alternative economy. Reclaiming every dollar of illegitimate debt service we hand over to the banks—a substantial chunk of all disposable income—and using it in genuinely beneficial and community-minded ways would go a long way to underwriting a sustainable, credit-for-use system.

Two months after the DROM was released, Strike Debt launched the Rolling Jubilee as an innovative example of debt relief. When loans do not "perform" within a set period of time (usually from ninety to 180 days), banks and other lenders are required to offload them. They are then sold for pennies on the dollar on the secondary markets, and the lenders are allowed to write them down for tax purposes as "losses." Collectors, many of them financed by the banks themselves, buy the debts very cheaply and try to collect on the full amount. The profit margin—the difference between sale price and collectable returns—is huge. This shadowy marketplace is populated by profiteers who ruthlessly exploit people's hardship and misfortune. The idea behind the Rolling Jubilee was to raise money to buy up and eliminate

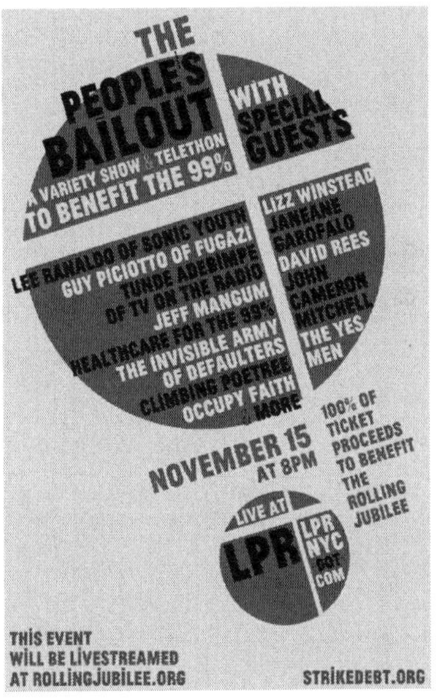

Promotional poster for *The People's Bailout: A Variety Show and Telethon to Benefit the 99 percent* (courtesy Le Poisson Rouge)

some of the discounted debt. Instead of collecting on the debt, as the collection agencies do, the project would abolish it, relieving debtors of all obligations. Launched through a telethon, billed as a "bailout by the people, for the people," it was presented to its crowdsourced funders as an opportunity to offer debtors some support and solidarity where the government had failed them. The Rolling Jubilee struck a chord with those who heard about it, and so it raised $500,000 in a matter of weeks ($635,000 before the fund was wound down in December 2013), which was ten times more than had been anticipated. Given how cheap it was to make the purchases, two-thirds of that sum proved to be enough to eliminate almost $15 million worth of debt in the course of one year. Instead of the expected 20:1 ratio, we were able to make buys that eliminated sums fifty times greater than the amount of money spent on purchases. Most of the abolished debts were medical, many of them generated from emergency room visits. People under extreme duress, with no other choices, had been saddled with hospital bills they simply could not pay.

Aside from helping hundreds of debtors, the project served to expose the predatory underpinnings of the marketplace in secondary debt. How many borrowers, hounded by collection agencies, knew how cheaply their harassers had bought out their loans? How many knew that the original lenders get to charge off their defaulted accounts as losses and take a tax break—another kind of bank bailout—before bundling the debts into portfolios for sale on the secondary market? Knowledge like this alters the psychology of debtors, providing moral ammunition for confronting collectors when they make their threatening phone calls. The viral circulation of the project guaranteed that this information reached a much larger population than the actual number of Rolling Jubilee debtors who received letters informing them they had been bailed out. For many who contributed to, or heard about, the project, the simple act of demonstrating that it was possible to abolish debt was an eye-opener, if not a meaningful breach of capitalist reality. Actions like this may have very limited practical consequences but they succeed in expanding our political imagination, constrained as it still is by the odious platitude that There Is No Alternative (TINA). The Rolling Jubilee was accomplished by ordinary people (most were small donors, whereas offers from larger institutional donors were turned down) helping others in trouble, and so it was also taken as an example of mutual aid in action.

The Rolling Jubilee team received tens of thousands of earnest messages from people whose spirits had been raised by the project. Hardened cynics might not have been moved by comments like the following:

"This gives me hope because I sincerely had none."

"I CRIED reading about your fundraiser."

"I have no money, but I could not not send in a dollar."

"THIS is the America I used to believe in. I'm ready to believe again!"

Though they might have been cheered by more militant ones like this:

"This is like a going-out-of-business sale at the 'Fuck Capitalism' store."

Rolling Jubilee digital meme, November 2012 (courtesy Strike Debt)

The Rolling Jubilee was designed as a small-scale public education project, and not in any way as a feasible solution to the debt crisis—the $15 million of abolished debt is barely a dent in the overall volume of the secondary debt market. Nonetheless, it attracted widespread attention from groups interested in using the concept for their own causes. Foremost among them were faith groups looking to revive the jubilee tradition among their own congregants and host communities. Some commentators also saw the Rolling Jubilee as an antidote to the vulture funds that buy distressed sovereign debts and sue to recover the full amount. Indeed, just one month before the Rolling Jubilee launch, Elliot Management, one of the most unscrupulous of these funds, seized an Argentinian naval vessel off the Ghanaian coast in its latest effort to force repayment of Argentinian bonds bought on the cheap after the government of that country defaulted in 2001. Shortly afterward, a New York court upheld Elliot's rights. Argentina's Economics Minister referred to the decision as "judicial colonialism," and the legal process, still under appeal, was tagged as the "sovereign debt trial of the century," with monumental implications for poor countries that had repudiated external debts taken on by kleptocratic leaders.

The vulture funds are highly vulnerable moral targets, regarded as pariahs because they expose all too readily the kind of practices that are standard business in the financial services industry. Yet only a difference of scale separates them from the buyers and collectors on the secondary debt market where the Rolling Jubilee team became a short-term player, and where rapacious conduct is routine. In that world, debtors are customarily hit up for debts they have long discharged, or else they are denied credit for payments; they are often threatened with bodily harm, lawsuits, arrest, prosecution, or imprisonment for nonpayment; and the sums they owe and the legal status of their debts are chronically misrepresented. After a long season of obstruction on the part of the GOP, the Consumer Financial Protection Bureau (CFPB), a watchdog agency created by the Dodd-Frank financial reform law, was finally permitted to set up shop. One of its first acts was to announce stronger scrutiny and prosecution of "unfair, deceptive, or abusive practices" in the debt collection industry—a multi-billion-dollar sector, involving more than 4,500 firms in the U.S.

If the CFPB is actually permitted to give some teeth to the regulation of this industry, then it will relieve some of the misery that is illegally inflicted on vulnerable debtors. But we should look forward to a day when the need for debt collectors is over. An economy where credit is available on the basis of social need and productive use must come to replace the current speculationist system of credit, enforced as it is by private intimidation and state coercion. Public regulation of the finance industry in its mature, royalist phase has been a spectacular failure.[11] It is delusional to believe that a twenty-first-century version of the Glass-Steagall Act, in the form of a ringfence or Chinese wall separating traditional retail banking from riskier investment banking, will regenerate fairness and decency in the world of finance. Bankers have shown that they have no real intention of abiding by the rules, and that they can afford to bribe every official who stands in their path.

Trying to imagine a macro-economy not driven by consumption growth or by capital accumulation can seem daunting, even for those who know that these twin imperatives distort and corrupt what most of us perceive as the common good. To some, the basic principles of de-growth—downscaling production and consumption toward a steady-state economy—may not sound credible enough to take a chance on. The economists who advocate for de-growth occupy a marginal niche on the landscape of professional and public opinion. Yet the elementary components of a cooperative successor economy already exist in a scattered, or piecemeal, state, in a variety of mutualist enterprises and non-profit credit initiatives. A good deal of what might be needed has already been invented, and is in use on a daily basis. While these practices exist "inside" of capitalism, they are non-capitalist at root.[12] Commons-based initiatives, in particular, are more and more preferred as the way forward, especially among anarchist-influenced groups who favor mutual aid concepts of the sort that emphasize cooperative conduct—really free markets, barter networks, community currencies, free cycle, time banks, gift economies, free stores, hacker spaces, community crowdfunding, co-housing, self-education.

Bank Transfer Day, on November 5, 2011, saw the launch of an Occupy-driven campaign for customers to switch bank accounts to credit unions. Whether they were disgusted by the fraud and greed displayed by Wall Street, or just turned off by increases in banking fees, a staggering 5.6 million big bank customers switched banks in the first ninety days.[13] As a result, membership in the 7200 U.S. credit unions has topped ninety-five million (with total assets of $1 trillion), and is rising rapidly. In the U.K., membership had reached one million in July 2013 before being boosted by the Archbishop of Canterbury's declaration of war against payday lenders. His call to open up branches of the Anglican Church to credit unions committed to proving alternative non-profit services even garnered support from the conservative coalition government.[14] In the U.S. a campaign is afoot to restore to the U.S. Postal Service the capacity to provide traditional banking services, primarily to the unbanked.[15]

Although mutual or cooperative savings banks, owned by members, were widely used in the nineteenth and twentieth centuries, deregulation in the 1980s saw most of them converted into stock ownership companies, mandated to deliver profits to shareholders. More innovative grassroots initiatives are poised to take their place. When the major banks bombard potential customers with promotional ads offering "free banking," the result is anything but. A truly free credit system would strive to create zero or near-to-zero interest loans to meet social needs such as the upfront costs of community ventures. The Occupy Bank Working Group has promoted the goal of creating a new kind of cooperative national bank, inspired by the ShoreBank, created in the 1970s, and once the largest certified community development financial institution in the U.S., before it failed during the financial crisis. In July 2013, the group launched Occupy Money Cooperative, along with a prototype of its first product, the Occupy Card, a pre-paid debit card that will provide an array of low-cost services.

Employee-owned companies (more than ten thousand in the U.S.) and workers' cooperatives are also enjoying a renaissance. Indeed, in 2012, the UN's International Year of the Cooperative, as many as 40 percent, or 130 million, Americans belonged to a co-op of some kind (29,000 in all), ranging from local businesses (grocery stores, coffee shops, movie theaters, daycare centers, artists, health care, taxi services) to large agricultural and electrical co-ops, and Fortune 500 companies like Associated Press, Land O' Lakes, Sunkist, Ace Hardware, and Ocean Spray. Most were stakeholder-based, and, cumulatively, they accounted for a significant share of the general economy. On the housing landscape, as many as five thousand community development corporations provide vital services and low-income housing built and managed on a non-profit basis. Community land trusts, with historic roots in the Garden City movement, help to sustain affordable housing, community gardens, and other civic buildings by staving off gentrification and preventing foreclosures on trust land. Community-supported agriculture (CSA) is a burgeoning alternative to the industrial food system, while the fair trade movement provides a market for producer cooperatives in developing countries.

Manufacturing cooperatives like the giant Mondragon federation (with more than 83,000 worker-members and one hundred affiliates) in the Basque country are models of industrial democracy and credit provision. In 2009, the United Steelworkers of America (USW), the mother of industrial unions, entered into alliance with Mondragon to create hybrid union/co-op organizations, funded by cooperative banks or credit unions with an interest in productive investment. The emergence of this partnership was a sweet postscript to the USW's opposition, in the 1970s, to Youngstown union members who tried to revive a shuttered steel mill and run it by themselves. The new alliance underlined how much the traditional, hierarchical union model had declined in the intervening years.[16] The *fábricas recuperadas* (recovered factories) movement in Argentina resulted in more than two hundred successful cooperatives after workers re-occupied workplaces that had been abandoned by owners after the 2001 economic crisis.[17] The Argentinian model of self-management proved an inspiration to locked-out workers in Greece and Spain, and, in the U.S., to employees of the former Republic Windows and Doors, which was revived as New Era, and opened for business again in May 2013. In the U.K., the birthplace of the co-op movement, the overall decline of co-ops was reversed from the 1980s, and they are thriving today, from new small-scale food enterprises to the retail giant, John Lewis Partners, the third largest private company in the U.K., and entirely employee-owned.

While viewed as marginal, and duly labeled as "heterodox," by mainstream economists, each of the forms of mutualism mentioned above has a long, functional history in societies around the world. They are influenced, if not entirely governed, by the principle that production is a common good, that credit should be accessible to all, and that workers and members are participants, beneficiaries, and equal partners with managers. While they operate within a capitalist system, and are subject to market pressures, they are not wholly governed by capitalist principles. Some see these alternatives as disparate examples, to use the anarchist phrase, of "building a new world within the shell of the old," though anarchists generally want much deeper, or more horizontal, vehicles of democracy than that provided by, say, an employee stock-ownership plan. Mondragon, for example, is worker-owned but not worker-managed. Self-organization, as a principle of strong participatory democracy, requires the constant assertion of transparency, shared input, and consensus. So, too, commoning—the practice of social cooperation for the use and conservation of common goods—thrives on the kind of inspired invention that an overly laborious democratic process can easily stifle.

Thirty years of neoliberalism in which the core power of the state has been commandeered to privatize public resources has soured younger people on the defense of public provision, and so there is less and less appetite for reconstituting the supply of basic needs in the form of public goods and services. Many of the initiatives mentioned above operate outside of the orbit of public provision, and are quite removed from the model of state authority. But there is no reason why the state should not be involved in the business of birthing alternative economies. Even if the hunger for commoning proves to be an ever-stronger source of change in the years to come, government powers and public provisioning will still be indispensable. Sweeping legislative changes will be required to break the stranglehold of the financial industry on government. As for banking itself, it is important to remember that banks are creations of the state, and that strong state action is needed to transform them into services that actually benefit communities.

Public option banking is one successor model that does not shirk from state ownership, and it is currently attracting a lot of attention. Although the federal government operates as many as 140 banks and quasi-banks for a variety of lending and subsidy purposes, public banking has not been a norm in the U.S, and so its potential for servicing community needs exudes a fresh appeal. Currently, the Bank of North Dakota is the only state-owned institution, and its ability to operate successfully in the public interest, not to mention its immunity to financial market failure, is revered among the state's staunchly conservative residents. Founded in 1919 when North Dakota farmers were losing their farms to Wall Street, the bank harnesses state revenues to offer affordable credit through credit unions and community banks. These non-profit entities make the kind of useful loans that are scorned by rent-seeking commercial and investment banks, and they return the interest to the state's general fund. The publicly-owned Alberta Treasury Branches in Canada have a similar performance record, while public banks in Europe control a huge chunk of the EU's assets. Almost all of the money is kept within the community, the costs of public goods and services are not inflated by high interest rates, and the common wealth is protected from being siphoned off for credit-default swaps and other risky investments.[18] Tired of being scammed by Wall Street's con games, officials in dozens of other states, counties, and cities are currently considering whether to set up similar publicly-owned and -operated banking enterprises. The Public Banking Institute was established in 2011 to promote this transition.

Aside from the potential of state-owned banking, we will continue to need public goods that are made universally available. The public provision of affordable education, healthcare, and housing is still the best guarantee of equity for large polities with socio-economically diverse populations. Just as important, any significant transition to low-carbon life will necessitate a shift toward renewable energy infrastructures that only state power and public institutions can deliver on a commensurate scale and within the requisite time frame. Putting solar panels on every roof and establishing community control over utilities are a good long-term goal for advocates of energy democracy, but large-scale measures, like government shutdowns of coal-fired power stations and levying of hefty carbon taxes, are urgently needed to reduce emissions and make sustainable alternatives cost-effective.

In brief, the likely upshot is that a new economy will be a mixed economy, not in the old sense of social democracy, or even market socialism, but one in which the public and the commons are more conversant and cooperative. Ideally, one will cede to the other, depending on which can deliver more democracy (not to be confused with efficiency) under any given circumstance. It may make more sense, for example, for a credit union to support the startup phase of a worker cooperative within the community, but a public bank might work better for that coop if it launched with branches, or parts of a supply chain, in different parts of a state.

LAST WORD, ON DEMOCRACY

Much of this book has touched on the claim that democracy has no tenable future unless creditor power is broken apart and dispersed. Popular trust in representative democracy has long been on the wane, and the rise of transnational corporations that pay little to no taxes has gutted the capacity of elected legislators to fairly allocate national distributions. Not surprisingly, people under the age of forty with no first-hand experience, nor any expectation, of robust social insurance have developed a sharp appetite for more direct forms of democracy. Indeed, their version of the American Dream is to live debt-free, whereas their grandparents may have welcomed debt as a gateway to the good life. At this point, they see government and high finance as too intertwined to separate. Self-organized and self-governing communities appear to be the preferred vehicles for their ideals. The new democracy movement that began in Tunisia in the winter of 2011, and spread to embrace the creative energies and allegiances of tens of millions across the world, proved that the hunger for such alternatives is widely shared.

For the *indignados* and *acampadas* assembled in Madrid's Puerta del Sol and other Spanish plazas, and the *aganaktismenoi* (outraged) who took over Athens' Syntagma Square, and the OWS cohort in Zuccotti Park and hundreds of other locations worldwide, it was not enough to expose the double standard that benefited economic oligarchs at the expense of the general populace. Blueprints for an alternative society had to be put on public display. Some substance had to be given to the slogan, borrowed from the global-justice movement—"This Is What Democracy Looks Like!"—which kept company with demands for "*Democracia Real YA!*" in Spain, "*Amesi Dimokratia Tora!*" in Greece, "Real Democracy Now!" in the U.K., Germany, and elsewhere—and the ubiquitous Arabic call to "bring down the regime": "*Ash-shab yurid isqat an-nizam!*" Peoples' assemblies (and spokes councils) based on decision-making by consensus offered the rare experience, and the breathtaking public spectacle, of face-to-face deliberation. The assemblies generated permission to speak openly and also to act autonomously in the labor-intensive meetings and actions of the myriad Occupy working groups.

The democratic experiment in micro community-building was just as vibrant. Under the spotlight of the world's media, occupiers transformed the privately-owned public space of Zuccotti Park into something like a commons, with communal kitchens, street medics, sanitation crews, social workers, a free university, and an array of quasi-municipal services in place.[19] Here, the principles of mutual aid were tried out, to the benefit of all who came to participate. Treatment of the unhoused, drawn in by the availability of food and respite from social disrespect, became the acid test of whether the park's prefigurative community could successfully accommodate the people whom capitalist society kicks to the margins.[20] Occupy had room for everyone, and some bad behavior was to be expected, given how many were "damaged by capitalism." Despite the ecumenical congregation, the overall tacit agreement was to play by the rules of anarchist conduct.[21] One prime lesson was that behaving like genuinely free people takes a good deal of training and discipline. This is especially true for direct action, involving likely confrontation with police repression, which many see as a necessary showdown with the unacceptably violent and illegitimate authority of the state.[22]

The outpouring of Occupy-flavored mass protests in Turkey and Brazil in 2013 demonstrated that the passion for real democracy was still proving to be "contagious," as David Graeber has put it. Each of these insurgencies has its own social composition, grievances, and local targets, but they share a common character—open, leaderless, populist, and consensual—that is often tagged as horizontalist. Adopted as a working concept in Argentina as part of the 2001 popular rebellions, horizontalism was quickly taken up as the house style of the global-justice movement. Its consensual process has particularly deep roots in the U.S., where scholars, researching the Indian roots of American democracy, can trace it to the Iroquois longhouse. Its place in the annals of Anglo communalism is usually tied to Quaker practice, and indeed, many of the protocols and rules for the Occupy general assemblies came out of the Quaker-inspired Clamshell Alliance of the 1970s and 1980s. Horizontal process also permeated the civil rights and women's movements, where it was adopted as an alternative to the top-down leadership culture of the Old Left.

At this point, it could be said that horizontalism has entered the customary lifeblood of society, but could it ever supplant the functions of representative democracy? Probably not any time soon, at least not beyond the scale of local assemblies. But it has become an entrenched generational habit, and will work its way, willy-nilly, into the civil conduct of the future. If this is what democracy really looks like, then the current version—governed by the Washington-Wall Street axis of debt—is something we should agree to call by the more accurate name of creditocracy. But name-calling is easy; the point, as Marx said, is to change it.

NOTES

INTRODUCTION

1. Yalman Onaran, "U.S. Banks Bigger Than GDP as Accounting Rift Masks Risk," *Bloomberg News* (Feb 19, 2013), accessible at http://www.bloomberg.com/news/2013-02-20/u-s-banks-bigger-than-gdp-as-accounting-rift-masks-risk.html.
2. See Nomi Prins, *All the Presidents' Bankers: The Hidden Alliances that Drive American Power* (New York: Avalon, 2013).
3. Letter to Col. Edward Mandell House (21 November 1933) in *F.D.R.: His Personal Letters, 1928-1945*, edited by Elliott Roosevelt (New York: Duell, Sloan and Pearce, 1950), p. 373.
4. As quoted in Robert Manning, *Credit Card Nation: The Consequences of America's Addiction to Credit Cards* (New York: Basic Books, 2000), p. 27.
5. According to an August 2013 report from the Federal Reserve Bank of New York, almost 15 percent of all credit reports—covering an estimated thirty million consumers—displayed collection items from debt collection. In other words, one in seven Americans was being, or had been, hounded by debt collectors. *Quarterly Report on Household Debt and Credit* (August 2013), accessible at http://www.newyorkfed.org/research/national_economy/householdcredit/DistrictReport_Q22013.pdf.
6. See Greta Krippner, *Capitalizing on Crisis: The Political Origins of the Rise of Finance* (Cambridge, Mass.: Harvard University Press, 2011); Costas Lapavitsas, *Profiting Without Producing: How Finance Exploits Us All* (London: Verso, 2014); Joseph Stiglitz, *The Price of Inequality: How Today's Divided Society Endangers Our Future* (New York: Norton, 2012); John Lanchester, *I.O.U.: Why Everyone Owes Everyone and No One Can Pay* (New York: Simon and Schuster, 2010); Michael Hudson, *The Bubble and Beyond: The Road from Industrial Capitalism to Finance Capitalism and Debt Peonage* (New York: Islet, 2012).

7. Matt Taibbi, "Greed and Debt: The True Story of Mitt Romney and Bain Capital," *Rolling Stone* (August 29, 2012).
8. "Striking it Richer: The Evolution of Top Incomes in the United States," a series of data reports by Emmanuel Saez and Thomas Piketty, outlines how the 1 percent have captured income growth. The first in the series was "Income Inequality in the United States, 1913-1998," *Quarterly Journal of Economics*, 118(1), 2003, 1-39. The most recent update can be found at http://elsa.berkeley.edu/~saez/saez-UStopincomes-2012.pdf, and it shows that the top 1 percent earners captured 95 percent of the income gains since the recession officially ended. Also see Josh Bivens and Lawrence Mishel, "The Pay of Corporate Executives and Financial Professionals as Evidence of Rents in Top 1 Percent Incomes," *Journal of Economic Perspectives* (Summer 2013), and Edward N. Wolff, "The Asset Price Meltdown and the Wealth of the Middle Class" (New York University, 2012), accessible at https://appam.confex.com/appam/2012/webprogram/Paper2134.html.
9. James MacDonald, *A Free Nation Deep in Debt: The Financial Roots of Democracy* (New York: Farrar, Straus & Giroux, 2003).
10. Bruce Mann, *Republic of Debtors: Bankruptcy in the Age of American Independence* (Cambridge, Mass.: Harvard University Press, 2003).
11. Thomas Jefferson, Letter to John W. Eppes (June 24, 1813), in William Parker and Jonas Viles, eds., *Letters and Addresses of Thomas Jefferson* (New York: Unit Books, 1905), p. 221.
12. Peter Eavis, "Cost Aside, JP Morgan May Have a Good Deal," *New York Times* (November 20, 2013).
13. Anat Admati and Martin Hellwig, *The Bankers' New Clothes: What's Wrong with Banking and What to Do About It* (Princeton: Princeton University Press, 2013), p. 2.
14. Damien Millet and Eric Toussaint, *Who Owes Who?: 50 Questions about World Debt* (London: Zed Books, 2004); and *Debt, the IMF, and the World Bank: Sixty Questions, Sixty Answers* (New York: Monthly Review Press, 2010).
15. François Chesnais, *Les dettes illégitimes: Quand les banques font main basse sur les politiques publiques* (Paris: Liber, 2012).
16. George Caffentzis, "Debt and/or Wages: Organizing Challenges," *Tidal* (February 2013).
17. Michael Hudson, "Democracy and Debt: Has the Link been Broken?" *Frankfurter Allgemeine Zeitung* (December 5, 2011) accessible in English at http://michael-hudson.com/2011/12/democracy-and-debt/.
18. Carmen Reinhart and Kenneth Rogoff, *This Time is Different: Eight Centuries of Financial Folly* (Princeton: Princeton University Press, 2009).
19. Marina Sitrin and Dario Azzelini, *They Can't Represent US! Reinventing Democracy from Greece to Occupy* (New York: Verso Press, 2013); Da-

vid Graeber, *The Democracy Project: A History, a Crisis, a Movement* (New York: Spiegel and Grau, 2013); Michael Hardt and Antonio Negri, *Declaration* (New York: Hardt and Negri, 2012); A.J. Bauer, Cristina Beltran, Rana Jaleel, and Andrew Ross, eds., *Is This What Democracy Looks Like?* (New York: Social Text, 2012), accessible at http://what-democracy-looks-like.com/.

20. Occupy Student Debt Campaign at http://www.occupystudentdebtcampaign.org and Strike Debt at www.strikedebt.org.

CHAPTER ONE

1. Michel Crozier, Samuel Huntington, and Joji Watanuki, *The Crisis of Democracy: Report on the Governability of Democracies to the Trilateral Commission* (New York: New York University Press, 1975).
2. See Noam Chomsky's analysis of the Trilateral Commission in "The Carter Administration: Myth and Reality," in *Radical Priorities* (Montreal: Black Rose Press, 1981).
3. "American Household Credit Card Debt Statistics: 2013," based on Federal Reserve data, accessible at http://www.nerdwallet.com/blog/credit-card-data/average-credit-card-debt-household/.
4. Historian Scott Reynolds Nelson's father was a repo man, hence the title of his book, *A Nation of Deadbeats: An Uncommon History of America's Financial Disasters* (New York, Knopf, 2012).
5. Jeff Madrick, "A Bit of Good News," *Harper's* (April 2013).
6. Craig Copeland, "Debt of the Elderly and Near Elderly, 1992–2010," Employment Benefit Research Institute, Vol. 34, No. 2 (February 2013), accessible at http://www.ebri.org/pdf/notespdf/EBRI_Notes_02_Feb-13_DebtEld-Contribs.pdf
7. Kelly Greene, "New Peril for Parents: Their Kids' Student Loans," *Wall Street Journal* (October 26, 2012).
8. Brett Williams, *Debt for Sale: A Social History of the Credit Trap* (Philadelphia: University of Pennsylvania Press, 2004).
9. Interview with Christian Marazzi by Ida Dominijanni, "The State of Debt—The Ethics of Guilt," *Il manifesto* (March 12, 2011), translated by Jason Francis McGimsey, in *Uninomade* (December 5, 2011), accessible at http://www.uninomade.org/state-of-debt-ethics-of-guilt/.
10. Maurizio Lazzarato, trans. Joshua David Jordan, *The Making of the Indebted Man* (New York: Semiotexte, 2012).
11. Neil Barosky, *Bailout: An Inside Account of How Washington Abandoned Main Street While Rescuing Wall Street* (New York: Free Press, 2012).
12. Ann Larson, "Cities in the Red: Austerity Hits America," *Dissent* (November 16, 2012). Matt Taibbi explains how the current municipal debt crisis

is also an outcome of officials diverting public pension funds into high-risk investments. "Looting the Pension Funds," *Rolling Stone* (September 26, 2013).

13. See the Protest and Assembly Rights report from legal clinics at Harvard, NYU, Stanford, and Fordham, *Suppressing Protest: Human Rights Violations in the U.S. Response to Occupy Wall Street* (July 25, 2012), accessible at http://chrgj.org/wp-content/uploads/2012/10/suppressingprotest.pdf. Also, see the Partnership for Civil Justice Fund report, "FBI Documents Reveal Secret Nationwide Occupy Monitoring" (December 22, 2012), accessible at http://www.justiceonline.org/commentary/fbi-files-ows.html.
14. Cheryl Payer gives a fuller picture in *The Debt Trap: The International Monetary Fund and the Third World* (New York: Monthly Review Press, 1974); and *The World Bank: A Critical Analysis* (New York: Monthly Review Press, 1982).
15. Manning, *Credit Card Nation*, p. 73.
16. Walden Bello, "Global Economic Counterrevolution: How Northern Economic Warfare Devastates the South," in Kevin Danaher, ed., *Fifty Years is Enough: The Case Against the World Bank and the International Monetary Fund* (Boston: South End Press, 1991).
17. Kathy McAfee, *Storm Signals: Structural Adjustment and Development Alternatives in the Caribbean* (London: Zed Books, 1991).
18. "Jamaica Agrees to $750m IMF Loan Terms," *The Guardian* (February 17, 2013).
19. Oscar Olivera and Tom Lewis, *¡Cochabamba! Water War in Bolivia* (Boston: South End Press, 2008).
20. Quoted in Eric Toussaint and Damien Millet, *Debt, the IMF, and the World Bank: Sixty Questions, Sixty Answers* (New York: Monthly Review Press, 2010), p. 178.
21. Federico Sturzenegger and Jeromin Zettelmeyer, *Debt Defaults and Lessons from a Decade of Crises* (Cambridge, Mass.: MIT Press, 2007).
22. Carmen Reinhart and Kenneth Rogoff, *This Time Is Different: Eight Centuries of Financial Folly* (Princeton; Princeton University Press, 2009), p. 30.
23. Renaud Vivien, Cécile Lamarque, "How Debts Can Legally Be Declared Void," Committee for the Abolition of Third World Debt (20 March, 2013), accessible at http://cadtm.org/How-debts-can-legally-be-declared.
24. Toussaint and Millet, p. 134.
25. The case for cancellation on moral, legal, economic, political, and environmental grounds is best laid out in Toussaint and Millet, pp. 240-60. Also see Patricia Adams, *Odious Debts: Loose Lending, Corruption, and the Third World's Environmental Legacy* (London: Earthscan, 1991).
26. Toussaint and Millet, pp. 26-27.

27. Toussaint and Millet, p. 155.
28. See Jubilee Debt's survey of the impact of debt and austerity, and campaigns for justice, in Egypt, El Salvador, Greece, Jamaica, Latvia, Pakistan, the Philippines, Portugal, and Tunisia, in Jeremy Dear, Paula Dear, and Tim Jones, *Life and Debt: Global Studies of Debt and Resistance* (London: Jubilee Debt, 2013).
29. Neil MacFarquhar, "Banks Making Big Profits From Tiny Loans," *New York Times* (April 13, 2010).
30. Susan George, *The Debt Boomerang: How Third World Debt Harms Us All* (Boulder, Co.: Westview Press, 1992).
31. Mark Blyth, *Austerity: The History of a Dangerous Idea* (New York: Oxford University Press, 2013).
32. Robert Kuttner, *Debtors' Prison: The Politics of Austerity Versus Possibility* (New York: Random House, 2013), p. 154.
33. Suzanne Daley, "As Germans Push Austerity, Greeks Press Nazi-Era Claims," *New York Times* (October 5, 2013). Syriza, the left opposition party, has championed the Greek Debt Audit Campaign that incorporates the war loan claims. See http://elegr.gr/details.php?id=323. For a good analysis of the austerity crisis, with particular insights into the Greek predicament, see Costas Lapavitsas, *Crisis in the Eurozone* (London: Verso, 2012).
34. "'Don't Owe, Won't Pay!': A Conversation with a French Debt Resistor," *Strike Debt* (June 24th, 2013), accessible at http://strikedebt.org/publicdebtaudits/ and International Citizen Debt Audit Network at http://www.citizen-audit.net/.

CHAPTER TWO

1. Alison Kilkenny, "A Slow-Motion Train Wreck: The Real Consequences of the Sequester," *The Nation* (June 24, 2013).
2. One such call came from Empowering and Strengthening Ohio's People. See http://www.esop-cleveland.org/index.php?option=com_content&view=article&id=124%3Ahomeowners-call-for-mortgage-strike&catid=8%3Ageneral&Itemid=46.
3. Hannah Appel and JP Massar, "Can a Small California City Take on Wall Street—And Survive?" *Strike Debt Bay Area* (September 29th, 2013), at http://strikedebt.org/em-dom-richmond/. Steven Lee Myers and Nicholas Kulish, "Growing Clamor About Inequities of Climate Crisis," *New York Times* (November 16, 2013).
4. John Lanchester, "Let's Consider Kate," *London Review of Books*, 35, 14 (July 18, 2013), p. 3.
5. Louis Hyman, *Borrow: The American Way of Debt* (New York: Vintage,

2012), pp. 44-52.

6. Stuart Ewen, *Captains of Consciousness: Advertising and the Social Roots of the Consumer Culture* (New York: McGraw-Hill, 1976).
7. Quoted in Louis Hyman, *Debtor Nation: The History of America in Red Ink* (Princeton: Princeton University Press, 2012), p. 43.
8. Herbert Hoover, "The Home as Investment," National Advisory Council for *Better Homes in America, Better Homes in America Plan Book for Demonstration Week October 9 to 14, 1922* (New York: Bureau of Information of Better Homes in America, 1922), p. 7.
9. For accounts of the conflict between thrift and consumerism, see Daniel Horowitz, *The Morality of Spending: Attitudes Toward the Consumer Society in America 1875-1940* (Baltimore: Johns Hopkins University Press, 1985); Lendol Calder, *Financing the American Dream: A Cultural History of Consumer Credit* (Princeton: Princeton University Press, 1999); and David Tucker, *The Decline of Thrift in America: Our Cultural Shift from Saving to Spending* (New York: Praeger, 1990).
10. Quoted in Hyman, *Debtor Nation*, p. 53.
11. John Lanchester, *I.O.U.: Why Everyone Owes Everyone and No One Can Pay*, p. 31.
12. Quoted in Kenneth Jackson, *Crabgrass Nation: The Suburbanization of the United States* (New York: Oxford University Press, 1985), p. 231.
13. Dolores Hayden, *Redesigning the American Dream: The Future of Housing, Work, and Family Life* (New York: Norton, 2002), pp. 49-50.
14. Rachel Bratt, Michael Stone, and Chester Hartman, eds., *A Right to Housing: Foundation for a New Social Agenda* (Philadelphia: Temple University Press, 2006).
15. Stanley Moses, "The Struggle for Decent Affordable Housing, Debates, Plans, and Policies," in *Affordable Housing in New York City: Definitions/Options* (New York: Steven Newman Real Estate Institute, Baruch University, 2005).
16. See Lizabeth Cohen, *A Consumers' Republic: The Politics of Mass Consumption in Postwar America* (New York: Vintage, 2003), p. 375-77. Also see Hyman, *Debtor Nation*, p. 180.
17. Cohen, *A Consumers' Republic.*
18. Paul Krugman, "Block Those Metaphors," *New York Times* (December 12, 2010).
19. Federal Reserve Bank of Saint Louis, "Households and Nonprofit Organizations; Credit Market Instruments; Liability, Level," accessible at http://www.research.stlouisfed.org/fred2/series/CMDEBT?cid=97.
20. Josh Bivens and Lawrence Mishel, "Occupy Wall Streeters Are Right About Skewed Economic Rewards in the United States," *Economic Policy Institute* (October 26, 2011), accessible at http://www.epi.org/publication/bp331-

occupy-wall-street/.

21. These estimates are compiled from data collected by the Federal Reserve's Household Debt Service and Financial Obligations Ratios, and are cited in David Graeber, *The Democracy Project*, p. 81.
22. See Strike Debt, *Debt Resistors' Operations Manual* (2012), chapters 7 and 8, accessible at http://strikedebt.org/The-Debt-Resistors-Operations-Manual.pdf. Howard Karger, *Shortchanged: Life and Debt in the Fringe Economy* (New York: Berrett-Koehler, 2005); and John Caskey, *Fringe Banking: Check-Cashing Outlets, Pawnshops, and the Poor* (New York: Russell Sage, 1994).
23. Ken Bensinger, "High Prices Are Driving More Motorists to Rent Tires," *Los Angeles Times* (June 8, 2013).
24. Gary Rivlin, *Broke, USA: From Pawnshops to Poverty, Inc.—How the Working Poor Became Big Business* (New York: HarperBusiness, 2010).
25. National People's Action, *Profiting from Poverty: How Payday Lenders Strip Wealth from the Working-Poor for Record Profits* (January 2012), accessible at http://npa-us.org/files/profiting_from_poverty_npa_payday_loan_report_jan_2012_0.pdf.
26. Jessica Silver-Greenberg and Stephanie Clifford, "Paid via Card, Workers Feel Sting of Fees," *New York Times* (June 30, 2013).
27. Alain Sherter, "As Economy Flails, Debtors' Prisons Thrive," *CBS MoneyWatch* (April 4, 2013), accessible at http://www.cbsnews.com/8301-505143_162-57577994/as-economy-flails-debtors-prisons-thrive/.
28. Matt Taibbi has vividly documented some of the many crimes in *Rolling Stone*: "Bank of America: Too Crooked to Fail" (March 14, 2011); "The Scam Wall Street Learned From the Mafia" (June 21, 2012); and "Everything Is Rigged: The Biggest Price-Fixing Scandal Ever" (April 25, 2013).
29. Bernie Sanders, "A Choice for Corporate America: Are You With America or the Cayman Islands?" *Huffington Post* (February 9, 2013), accessible at http://www.huffingtonpost.com/rep-bernie-sanders/a-choice-for-corporate-am_b_2652176.html.
30. James Felkerson, "$29,000,000,000,000: A Detailed Look at the Fed's Bail-out by Funding Facility and Recipient," Levy Economics Institute, Bard College, Working Paper No. 698 (December 2011), accessible at http://www.levyinstitute.org/publications/?docid=1462.
31. David Cole, *Enemy Aliens: Double Standards and Constitutional Freedoms in the War on Terrorism* (New York: New Press, 2003); Jane Mayer, *The Dark Side: The Inside Story of How The War on Terror Turned into a War on American Ideals* (New York: Doubleday, 2008); David Shipler, *The Rights of the People: How Our Search for Safety Invades Our Liberties* (New York: Knopf, 2011); and Shipler, *Rights at Risk: The Limits of Liberty in Modern America* (New York: Knopf, 2012).
32. Maude Barlow and Tony Clarke, *Global Showdown: How the New Activists*

Are Fighting Global Corporate Rule (Toronto: Stoddard, 2002) and Lori Wallach and Patrick Woodall, *Whose Trade Organization? The Comprehensive Guide to the WTO* (New York: New Press, 2004).

33. David Graeber, *Debt: The First 5000 Years* (New York: Melville Press, 2011); Peter Linebaugh, "Jubilating, or How the Atlantic Working Class Used the Biblical Jubilee against Capitalism, with Some Success," *Radical History Review* 50 (1991), pp. 143–80; Michael Hudson, "The Lost Tradition of Biblical Debt Cancellations," (New York: Henry George School of Social Science, 1992), accessible at http://michael-hudson.com/wp-content/uploads/2010/03/HudsonLostTradition.pdf.
34. Charles Geisst, *Beggar Thy Neighbor: A History of Usury and Debt* (Philadelphia: University of Pennsylvania Press, 2013).
35. Michelle Alexander, *The New Jim Crow: Mass Incarceration in the Age of Colorblindness* (New York: New Press, 2011).
36. Carmen Reinhart and Kenneth Rogoff, "Growth in a Time of Debt," *National Bureau of Economic Research*, Working Paper No. 15639 (January 2010).
37. Thomas Herndon, Michael Ash, and Robert Pollin, "Does High Public Debt Consistently Stifle Economic Growth? A Critique of Reinhart and Rogoff," *Political Economy Research Institute*, University Of Massachusetts, Amherst (April 15, 2013), accessible at http://www.peri.umass.edu/236/hash/31e2ff374b6377b2ddec04deaa6388b1/publication/566/.
38. Carmen Reinhart and Kenneth Rogoff, "Debt, Growth and the Austerity Debate," *New York Times* (April 25, 2013).
39. Michael Hardt and Antonio Negri, *Declaration* (New York: Hardt and Negri, 2012).
40. Robert Kuttner, *Debtor's Prison: The Politics of Austerity Versus Possibility* (New York: Knopf, 2013), p. 225.

CHAPTER THREE

1. Michael Crozier et al, *The Crisis of Democracy*, p. 191.
2. Phil Oliff, Vincent Palacios, Ingrid Johnson, and Michael Leachman, "Recent Deep State Higher Education Cuts May Harm Students and the Economy for Years to Come," Center for Budget and Policy Priorities (March 19, 2013), accessible at http://www.cbpp.org/cms/?fa=view&id=3927. Dylan Matthews offers a overview of the reasoning behind rising college costs, but downplays state cuts in his haste to promote the thesis that nonprofits are just too profligate in their appetite for spending. "The Tuition is Too Damn High," *Washington Post* (August 26—September 6, 2013), accessible at http://tinyurl.com/mugm527.
3. Elizabeth Warren and John Tierney, "Treat Students Like Banks," *Moyers and Company* (June 12, 2013), accessible at http://billmoyers.com/groupthink/

what-to-do-about-student-loans/the-bank-on-students-loan-fairness-act/.

4. Alan Collinge details the many crimes of Sallie Mae in *The Student Loan Scam: The Most Oppressive Debt in U.S. History and How We Can Fight Back* (Boston: Beacon Press, 2009).
5. The list of bills also included The Student Loan Fairness Act (H.R. 1330); The Student Loan Affordability Act (S. 707); The Student Loan Default Prevention Act (H.R. 618); The Know Before You Owe Private Student Loan Act (S. 113); The Student Loan Employment Benefits Act (H.R. 395); The Student Loan Interest Deduction Act (H.R. 1527); Responsible Student Loan Solutions Act (S. 909/H.R. 1946); The Student Loan Relief Act (S. 953); The Federal Student Loan Refinancing Act (S. 1066); Refinancing Education Funding to Invest for the Future Act (S.1266); Proprietary Institution of Higher Education Accountability Act (H.R.1928); Smarter Borrowing Act (S. 546); Students First Act of 2013 (S. 406).
6. Greg Kaufmann, "Taking On Sallie Mae and the Cost of Education," *The Nation* (May 31, 2013); Sarita Gupta, "Sallie Mae's Profits Soaring at the Expense of Our Nation's Students," *Moyers and Company* (June 12, 2013), accessible at http://tinyurl.com/kshvan3.
7. Jeremy Brecher, *Strike!* (Boston: South End Press, 1977, revised edition), pp. 243, 246, citing Art Preis, *Labor's Giant Step: Twenty Years of the CIO* (New York: Pioneer Publishers, 1964), p. 236; and Joel Seidman, *American Labor from Defense to Reconversion* (Chicago: University of Chicago Press, 1953), p. 235.
8. Richard Lewontin, "The Cold War and the Transformation of the Academy," in Noam Chomsky et al, *The Cold War and the University: Toward an Intellectual History of the Postwar Years* (New York: New Press, 1997).
9. Annual Report of the Consumer Financial Protection Bureau Student Loan Ombudsman (October 16, 2013), accessible at http://www.consumerfinance.gov/reports/.
10. Eric Dillon, "Leading Lady: Sallie Mae and the Origin of Today's Student Loan Controversy" (Washington DC: Education Sector, 2007), p.7.
11. Aaron Bady and Mike Konczal, "From Master Plan to No Plan: The Slow Death of Public Higher Education," *Dissent* (Fall 2012).
12. Health, Education, Labor, and Pensions Committee, U.S. Senate, *For Profit Higher Education: The Failure to Safeguard the Federal Investment and Ensure Student Success* (July 30, 2010).
13. Deborah Frankle Cochrane and Robert Shireman, "Denied: Community College Students Lack Access to Affordable Loans," *The Project on Student Debt* (April 2008), accessible at http://projectonstudentdebt.org/files/pub/denied.pdf.
14. Consumer Financial Protection Bureau, *Private Student Loans*, A Report to the Senate Committee on Banking, Housing, and Urban Affairs, the

Senate Committee on Health, Education, Labor, and Pensions, the House of Representatives Committee on Financial Services, and the House of Representatives Committee on Education and the Workforce (August 29, 2012), p. 36.

15. A subsequent CFPB investigation was launched into the flourishing payola practices whereby banks partner with colleges willing to grant them exclusive marketing of financial products to students; student ID cards, for example, that also function as debit cards, generating exorbitant fees. See Consumer Financial Protection Bureau, "Request for Information Regarding Financial Products Marketed to Students Enrolled in Institutions of Higher Education," accessible at http://tinyurl.com/pnrkzcr. Or Shahien Nasiripour, "Lawmakers Probe Big Banks Using Colleges To Target Students," *Huffington Post* (September, 27, 2013), accessible at http://www.huffingtonpost.com/2013/09/27/college-debit-cards_n_4004692.html.
16. Sandy Baum and Patricia Steele, "Who Borrows Most? Bachelor's Degree Recipients with High Levels of Student Debt," *College Board* (2010), p. 6, accessible at http://tinyurl.com/DROMBaum.
17. Julianne Hing, "Study: Only 37 Percent of Students Can Repay Loans on Time," *Colorlines* (March 17, 2011), accessible at http://tinyurl.com/DROMHing.
18. Hollister Petraeus, "For-Profit Colleges, Vulnerable G.I.'s," *New York Times* (September 21, 2011); Tamar Lewin, "Obama Signs Order to Limit Aggressive College Recruiting of Veterans," *New York Times* (April 27, 2012).
19. Adam Weinstein, "How Pricey For-Profit Colleges Target Vets' GI Bill Money," *Mother Jones* (September 2011).
20. Eric Lichtblau, "With Lobbying Blitz, For-Profit Colleges Diluted New Rules," *New York Times* (December 9, 2011).
21. Sam Ro, "How Student Debt Tripled in 8 Years, and Why It's Becoming a Growing Economic Problem," *Business Insider* (February 28, 2013), accessible at http://www.businessinsider.com/ny-fed-student-loans-presentation-2013-2?op=1#ixzz2YfEDysLd.
22. Malcolm Harris, "Bad Education," *n+1* (April 2011), accessible at http://nplusonemag.com/bad-education.
23. R. Simon, R. Ensign, and A. Yoon, "Student-Loan Securities Stay Hot," *Wall Street Journal* (March 3, 2013).
24. Jordan Weissmann, "Don't Panic: Wall St.'s Going Crazy for Student Loans, But This Is No Bubble," *The Atlantic* (March 4, 2013).
25. Under the rubric of Student Debt Forgiveness to Stimulate the Economy, Robert Applebaum collected a million signatures as part of a petition to

support the Student Loan Forgiveness Act of 2012. See "The Proposal" (January 29, 2009), accessible at http://www.forgivestudentloandebt.com/content/proposal.

26. "We Are the 99 percent" at http://wearethe99percent.tumblr.com/. In its first annual report, the CFPB compiled three thousand complaints about student loans after inviting the public to comment. The report is accessible at http://files.consumerfinance.gov/f/201210_cfpb_Student-Loan-Ombudsman-Annual-Report.pdf.
27. Cryn Johannsen, high-profile blogger and commentator on student debt, reflects on the suicide notes sent to her by student debtors in "National Emergency? Suicidal Student Debtors," *All Education Matters* (June 17, 2012), accessible at http://alleducationmatters.blogspot.com/2012/06/suicidal-debtors-is-national-emergency.html.
28. Peter Jacobs, "America's REAL Most Expensive Colleges," *Business Insider* (July 10, 2013), accessible at http://www.businessinsider.com/most-expensive-colleges-in-america-2013-7?op=1#ixzz2YqBs7t9r.
29. Benjamin Ginsberg, *The Fall of the Faculty: The Rise of the All-Administrative University and Why It Matters* (New York: Oxford University Press, 2011).
30. Douglas Belkin and Scott Thurm, "Deans List: Hiring Spree Fattens College Bureaucracy—And Tuition," *Wall Street Journal* (December 28, 2012).
31. See Bob Meister's open letter to UC students, "They Pledged Your Tuition to Wall Street," *Keep California's Promise* (October 2009), accessible at http://keepcaliforniaspromise.org/383/they-pledged-your-tuition.
32. Belkin and Thurm.
33. Andrew Ross, "Universities and the Urban Growth Machine," *Dissent* (October 4, 2012).
34. Faculty Against the Sexton Plan, *While We Were Sleeping: NYU and the Destruction of New York* (New York: McNally-Jackson, 2012), and more analysis of the NYU expansion plan can be found at http://nyufasp.com/.
35. Michael Denning, "The Fetishism of Debt," Dossier on Debt, *Social Text* (Periscope), (September 2011), accessible at http://www.socialtextjournal.org/periscope/going-into-debt/.
36. Tola Adewola, "Cuomo's Code of Conduct: Troubled Times for the Student Loan Industry," *Illinois Business Law Journal*, (April 24 2007); Pam Martens and Russ Martens, "The Untold Story of Citibank's Student Loan Deals at NYU," *Wall Street on Parade*, (September 16, 2013), accessible at http://wallstreetonparade.com/2013/09/the-untold-story-of-citibankpercentE-2percent80percent99s-student-loan-deals-at-nyu/.
37. Ariel Kaminer and Alain Delaqueriere, "N.Y.U. Gives Its Stars Loans for Summer Home," *New York Times* (June 17, 2013); Pam Martens, "NYU's Gilded Age: Students Struggle With Debt While Vacation Homes Are

Lavished on the University's Elite" (June 17, 2013); and "NYU Channels Wall Street: New Documents Show Lavish Pay, Perks and Secret Deals" (June 10, 2013), accessible at *Wall Street on Parade* (http://wallstreetonparade.com/).

38. British Council, *Going Global 2012*, accessible at http://ihe.britishcouncil.org/sites/default/files/going_global/session_attachments/GG2012%20 12.1%20Janet%20Illieva.pdf. In 2009, John Hudzik, president of NAFSA Association of International Educators, forecast 80 percent growth over the next decade. Demand would grow to as many as two hundred million "seats" by the year 2020—students enrolled at that time, in his estimate, numbered from 110 to 115 million. See Elizabeth Redden, "In Global Recession, Global Ed Still Growing," in *Inside Higher Ed* (May 29, 2009), accessible at http://www.insidehighered.com/news/2009/05/29/international.
39. Andrew Ross, "Human Rights, Academic Freedom, and Offshore Academics," *Academe* (January-February, 2011); and "Away from Home: The Case of University Employees Overseas," *South Atlantic Quarterly*, 108, 4 (2009); Jackson Diehl, "Yale, NYU Sacrifice Academic Freedom," *Washington Post* (June 23, 2013).
40. A similar belief underpins the expansion of income-based repayment, as proposed by the Obama administration, and, to some degree, the Pay It Forward plan adopted by the Oregon legislature in July 2013, which offers a system of tuition-free education upfront, to be funded after graduation in income-based repayment. Sarah Jaffe summarizes the debate about the Oregon development: "Perhaps the biggest—and least tangible—question is whether the Pay It Forward plan is a shift back toward a view of higher education as something that benefits the entire society and should be paid for, progressively, by the entire society, or whether it is a further embrace of the neoliberal idea that education is a personal investment that should be paid for by the individual. "A Debt-Free Degree?" *In These Times* (August 7, 2013).
41. Robert Samuels, *Why Public Higher Education Should Be Free: How to Decrease Cost and Increase Quality at American Universities* (New Brunswick: Rutgers University Press, 2013). Also see Mike Konczal, "Could We Redirect Tax Subsidies to Pay for Free College?" *Next New Deal* (December 20, 2011), accessible at http://www.nextnewdeal.net/rortybomb/could-weredirect-tax-subsidies-pay-free-college; and Jordan Weissmann, "How Washington Could Make College Tuition Free (Without Spending a Penny More on Education)," *The Atlantic* (March 8, 2013).
42. Strike Debt, "How Far to Free?" (August 15th, 2013), accessible at http://strikedebt.org/how-far-to-free/; and Ann Larson and Michael Cheque, "Higher Education Can Be Free," *Jacobin*, accessible at http://jacobinmag.

com/2013/09/higher-education-can-be-free/.

43. Cited in Alternative Banking Group of Occupy Wall Street, *Occupy Finance* (2013), p. 13. At http://www.scribd.com/doc/168661471/Occupy-Finance.
44. William Baumol and William Bowen, *Performing Arts, The Economic Dilemma: A Study of Problems Common to Theater, Opera, Music, and Dance* (New York: Twentieth Century Fund, 1966). William Bowen, in *The Economics of the Major Private Universities*, Carnegie Commission on Higher Education (New York: McGraw-Hill, 1968), draws on the cost disease model to analyze higher education in particular.
45. Rudy Fichtenbaum and Hank Reichman, "Obama's Rankings Won't Solve Crisis in US Academy," *Times Higher Education Supplement* (12 September 2013). Also, see the data collected by the Delta Cost Project at the American Institutes for Research, at http://www.deltacostproject.org/.
46. William J. Baumol et al, *The Cost Disease: Why Computers Get Cheaper and Health Care Doesn't* (New Haven, CT: Yale University Press, 2012).
47. See the Hamilton Project's report, "Regardless of the Cost, College Still Matters," Brookings Institution, accessible at http://www.hamiltonproject.org/papers/Regardless_of_the_Cost_College_Still_Matters/.
48. The Georgetown Public Policy Institute estimate of $2.7 million can be found at Anthony P. Carnevale, Stephen J. Rose, and Ban Cheah, "The College Payoff: Education, Occupations, Lifetime Earnings" (August 5, 2011), accessible at http://www9.georgetown.edu/grad/gppi/hpi/cew/pdfs/collegepayoff-complete.pdf. The Pew Research Center estimate of $650,000 is by D'Vera Cohn, "Lifetime Earnings of College Graduates" (May 16, 2011), accessible at http://www.pewsocialtrends.org/2011/05/16/lifetime-earnings-of-college-graduates/.
49. Robert Hiltonsmith, "At What Cost? How Student Debt Reduces Lifetime Wealth," *Demos* (August 1, 2013), accessible at http://www.demos.org/what-cost-how-student-debt-reduces-lifetime-wealth.
50. Bob Meister, "Debt and Taxes: Can the Financial Industry Save Public Universities?" *Representations*, 116 (Fall 2011).
51. Michael Sandel, *What Money Can't Buy: The Moral Limits of Markets* (New York: Farrar, Straus & Giroux, 2012).
52. The literature on this topic is immense, from Thorstein Veblen's jeremiad against the "pecuniary" culture in *The Higher Learning In America: A Memorandum on the Conduct of Universities by Business Men* (New York: B. W. Huebsch, 1918) to the 2004 analysis of academia as a vehicle of capital formation in Sheila Slaughter and Gary Rhoades, *Academic Capitalism and the New Economy: Markets, State, and Higher Education* (Baltimore: Johns Hopkins University Press, 2009).

CHAPTER FOUR

1. Steve Fraser, "The Politics of Debt in America: From Debtor's Prison to Debtor Nation," *Jacobin* (February 4, 2013).
2. Chris Noon, "Berkshire Hathaway CEO Blasts 'Sharecropper's Society,'" *Forbes Magazine* (March, 7, 2005).
3. Ben Stein, "In Class Warfare, Guess Which Class Is Winning?" *New York Times* (November 26, 2006).
4. Andrew Frye, "Munger Says 'Thank God' U.S. Opted for Bailouts Over Handouts," *Huffington Post* (September 20, 2010), accessible at http://www.bloomberg.com/news/2010-09-20/berkshire-s-munger-says-cash-strapped-should-suck-it-in-not-get-bailout.html.
5. Jeff Williams launched this line of inquiry in his essay, "Student Debt and The Spirit of Indenture," *Dissent* (Fall, 2008), pp. 73-78.
6. David Blacker, *The Falling Rate of Learning and the NeoLiberal Endgame* (London: Zero Books, 2013), p. 133.
7. Or, as activist Aaron Calafato did, by taking a job as an admissions officer at a for-profit college—paying off his debt by recruiting others into a debt trap. See Patricia Sabga, "Putting a Face on the Student Debt Crisis," *Al-Jazeera America* (September 19, 2013), accessible at http://america.aljazeera.com/watch/shows/real-money-with-alivelshi/Real-Money-Blog/2013/9/19/putting-a-face-onthestudentdebtcrisis.html.
8. William Alden, "Lending Start-Up CommonBond Raises $100 Million, With Pandit as Investor," *New York Times* (September 4, 2013). Also see Anand Reddi and Andreas Thyssen, "Healthcare Reform: Solving the Medical Student Debt Crisis Through Human Capital Contracts," *Huffington Post* (June 10th, 2011), accessible at http://www.huffingtonpost.com/anand-reddi/healthcare-reform-solving_b_874651.html.
9. Richard Dienst, *The Bonds of Debt: Borrowing Against the Common Good* (New York: Verso, 2009).
10. Tiziana Terranova, "Free Labor" and Andrew Ross, "In Search of the Lost Paycheck," in Trebor Scholz, ed., *Digital Labor: The Internet as Playground and Factory* (New York: Routledge, 2013); Mark Banks, Rosalind Gill, Stephanie Taylor, eds., *Theorizing Cultural Work: Labour, Continuity and Change in the Cultural and Creative Industries* (London: Routledge, 2013); David Hesmondhalgh and Sarah Baker, *Creative Labour: Media Work in Three Cultural Industries* (Abingdon and New York: Routledge, 2010).
11. Ross Perlin, *Intern Nation: How to Earn Nothing and Learn Little in the Brave New Economy* (New York: Verso, 2011).
12. Kim Bobo, in *Wage Theft in America: Why Millions of Working Americans Are Not Getting Paid—And What We Can Do About It* (New York: New Press, 2009) estimated that wage theft was netting employers at least $100 billion a year.

13. Annette Bernhardt et al, *Broken Laws, Unprotected Workers: Violations of Employment and Labor Laws in America's Cities* (New York: National Employment Law Project, 2009).
14. Gary Rivlin, *Broke USA: From Pawnshops to Poverty, Inc.—How the Working Poor Became Big Business* (New York: HarperBusiness, 2011). Barbara Ehrenreich, "Preying on the Poor: How Government and Corporations Use the Poor as Piggy Banks," Economic Hardship Reporting Project (May 17, 2012), accessible at http://economichardship.org/preying-on-the-poor/.
15. Mike Elk and Bob Sloan, "The Hidden History of ALEC and Prison Labor," *The Nation* (August 1, 2011); Steve Fraser and Joshua B. Freeman, "Locking Down an American Workforce," *Huffington Post* (April 20, 2012), accessible at http://www.huffingtonpost.com/steve-fraser/private-prisons-_b_1439201.html.
16. Marc Bousquet, *How the University Works: Higher Education and the Low-Wage Nation* (New York: NYU Press).
17. Michael Denning, "The Fetishism of Debt."
18. Alex Wayne, "Health-Care Spending to Reach 20 percent of U.S. Economy by 2021," *Bloomberg News* (June 13, 2012), accessible at http://www.bloomberg.com/news/2012-06-13/health-care-spending-to-reach-20-of-u-s-economy-by-2021.html.
19. Victor Fuchs, "The Gross Domestic Product and Health Care Spending," *New England Journal of Medicine*, 369 (July 11, 2013), pp. 107-9.
20. Strike Debt, *Death By For-Profit Health Care* (February 2013), accessible at http://strikedebt.org/medicaldebtreport/.
21. Mark Brenner, "Pension Theft Crime Wave," *Labor Notes* (October 21, 2013).
22. David Himmelstein, Deborah Thorne, Elizabeth Warren, and Steffie Woolhandler, "Medical Bankruptcy in the United States, 2007: Results of a National Study," *The American Journal of Medicine* (2009).
23. David Himmelstein, Deborah Thorne, Steffie Woolhandler, "Medical Bankruptcy in Massachusetts: Has Health Reform Made a Difference?" *American Journal of Medicine*, 124, 3 (March 2011), pp. 224-28.
24. José Garcia and Mark Rukavina, "Sick and in the Red: Medical Debt and its Economic Impact," *Demos/The Access Project* (March 26, 2013), accessible at http://www.accessproject.org/new/pages/item110.php.
25. David Blacker, *The Falling Rate of Learning,* p. 140.
26. Daniel Rodgers, *The Work Ethic in Industrial America, 1850-1920* (Chicago: University of Chicago Press, 1978).
27. Greenspan's comments are cited by Michael Hudson, in *Finance Capitalism and Its Discontents* (Dresden: Islet, 2012), p. 163.
28. Adolph Reed, "Majoring in Debt," *The Progressive* (January, 2004).

29. Jackie Tortora, "Trumka: Unions and Student Activists Share Similar Vision for America," *AFL-CIO Now* (July 26, 2012), accessible at http://www.aflcio.org/Blog/Other-News/Trumka-Unions-and-Student-Activists-Share-Similar-Vision-for-America.
30. Daniel Pink, *Free Agent Nation: The Future of Working for Yourself* (New York: Warner, 2001); Andrew Ross, *No-Collar: the Humane Workplace and Its Hidden Costs* (New York: Basic Books, 2003).
31. Richard Florida, *The Rise of The Creative Class: And How It's Transforming Work, Leisure and Everyday Life* (New York: Basic Books, 2002); and *Cities and the Creative Class* (New York: Routledge, 2005). Jamie Peck, "Struggling with the Creative Class," *International Journal of Urban and Regional Research*, 29, 4 (December 2005), pp. 740–70. Andrew Ross, *Nice Work If You Can Get It: Life and Labor in Precarious Times* (New York: NYU Press, 2009).
32. Richard Vedder, Christopher Denhart, and Jonathan Robe, *Why are Recent College Graduates Underemployed? University Enrollments and Labor Market Realities*, Center for College Affordability and Productivity (January 2013).
33. "Knowledge and Skills for the Jobs of the Future" on the White House website, accessible at http://www.whitehouse.gov/issues/education/higher-education. Michelle Obama has also been drafted into this campaign. See Jennifer Steinhauer, "Michelle Obama Edges Into a Policy Role on Higher Education," *New York Times* (November 11, 2013).
34. See Stephen Marche, "The War Against Youth," *Esquire* (March 26, 2012).
35. See Tamara Draut, *Strapped: Why America's 20- and 30-Somethings Can't Get Ahead* (New York: Doubleday, 2006).

CHAPTER FIVE

1. Potsdam Institute for Climate Impact Research and Climate Analytics, *Turn Down the Heat: Why a 4°C Warmer World Must be Avoided*, World Bank Working Paper 74455 (Washington DC: World Bank, December 19, 2012), accessible at http://climatechange.worldbank.org/sites/default/files/Turn_Down_the_heat_Why_a_4_degree_centrigrade_warmer_world_must_be_avoided.pdf; and *Turn Down the Heat: Climate Extremes, Regional Impacts, and the Case for Resilience* (Washington DC: World Bank, June 2013), accessible at http://documents.worldbank.org/curated/en/2013/06/17862361/turn-down-heat-climate-extremes-regional-impacts-case-resilience-full-report.
2. See Andrew Simms, Aubrey Meyer, Nick Robbins, *Who Owes Who?: Climate Change, Debt, Equity and Survival* (London: Christian Aid, 1999).
3. Joan Martinez-Allier, *The Environmentalism of the Poor: A Study of Ecological Conflicts and Valuation* (New York: Edward Elgar, 2002).

4. James Hansen, "Letter to Kevin Rudd" (March 27, 2008), accessible at http://www.aussmc.org.au/documents/Hansen2008LetterToKevin-Rudd_000.pdf. The breakdown was based on estimates from the Carbon Dioxide Information Analysis Center of the U.S. Department of Energy.
5. These assessments can be found at *Climate Debt, Climate Credit,* accessible at https://sites.google.com/site/climatedebtclimatecredit/net-climate-debt.
6. Eli Kintisch, *Hack the Planet: Science's Best Hope—or Worst Nightmare—for Averting Climate Catastrophe* (New York: Wiley, 2010).
7. The 150 million figure was first estimated by Norman Myers and Jennifer Kent, "Environmental Exodus: an Emergent Crisis in the Global Arena" (Washington DC: Climate Institute, 1995); and Myers, "Environmental Refugees: Our Latest Understanding," *Philosophical Transactions of the Royal Society,* Vol. 356 (2001), pp. 16.1-16.5. *The Stern Review: The Economics of Climate Change,* commissioned from economist Nicholas Stern by the U.K. government in 2006, put the figure at two hundred million. See also Environmental Justice Foundation, *No Place Like Home: Where Next For Climate Refugees?* (London: Environmental Justice Foundation, 2009).
8. International Federation of Red Cross and Red Crescent Societies, *World Disasters Report* (2010).
9. Andrew Ross, *Bird on Fire: Lessons from the World's Least Sustainable City* (New York: Oxford University Press, 2011).
10. Rob Nixon, *Slow Violence and the Environmentalism of the Poor* (Cambridge, Mass.: Harvard University Press, 2012); Frederick Buell, *From Apocalypse to Way of Life: Environmental Crisis in the American Century (New York:* Routledge, 2003).
11. U.S. Department of Defense, *Quadrennial Defense Review* (2010), accessible at http://www.defense.gov/qdr.
12. Peter Schwartz and Doug Randall, *An Abrupt Climate Change Scenario and Its Implications for United States National Security* (Emeryville, CA: Global Business Lab, 2003).
13. Rebecca Solnit, *A Paradise Built in Hell: The Extraordinary Communities That Arise in Disaster* (New York: Viking, 2009), p. 3.
14. Naomi Klein, *The Shock Doctrine: The Rise of Disaster Capitalism* (New York: Metropolitan Books/Henry Holt, 2007).
15. Strike Debt, *Shouldering the Costs: Who Pays in the Aftermath of Sandy?* accessible at http://strikedebt.org/sandyreport/.
16. Kevin Fox Gotham and Miriam Greenberg, "From 9/11 to 8/29: Post-Disaster Recovery and Rebuilding in New York and New Orleans," *Social Forces,* 87, 2 (December 2008), pp. 1039-62.
17. Cedric Johnson, *The Neoliberal Deluge: Hurricane Katrina, Late Capitalism, and the Remaking of New Orleans* (Minneapolis MN: University of

Minnesota Press, 2011); Daniel Wolff, *The Fight for Home: How (Parts of) New Orleans Came Back* (New York: Bloomsbury, 2012).

18. The choice is further complicated by the New York City Housing Authority's infill program, which will allow luxury development in the green space between public housing towers. The new housing will be built to meet FEMA's flood-resistant provisions, and will sit cheek by jowl with the vulnerable towers, magnifying the socio-economic divisions between their respective inhabitants.
19. NYC Special Initiative for Rebuilding and Resiliency, "A Stronger, More Resilient New York" (June 2013), accessible at http://www.nyc.gov/html/sirr/html/report/report.shtml.
20. See the city maps produced by the Robert Wood Johnson's Commission to Build a Healthier America, accessible at http://www.rwjf.org/en/about-rwjf/newsroom/features-and-articles/Commission/resources/city-maps.html.
21. Mike Davis, "Who Will Build the Ark," *New Left Review*, 61 (January-February 2010); Kent Portney, *Taking Sustainable Cities Seriously: Economic Development, the Environment, and Quality of Life in American Cities* (Cambridge, Mass: MIT Press, 2002).
22. Juliet Eilperin, "U.S. Climate Aid Reaches Across Globe," *Washington Post* (December 2, 2012).
23. Taryn Fransen and Smita Nakhooda, "Five Insights from Developed Countries' Fast-Start Finance Contribution," *Open Climate Network*, World Resources Institute (June 11, 2013), accessible at http://insights.wri.org/open-climate-network/2013/06/5-insights-developed-countries-fast-start-finance-contributions#sthash.r8XoOehl.dpuf.
24. See the special issue on "The Climate Debt: Who Profits, Who Pays?" *Report on the Americas*, North American Congress on Latin America, 46, 1 (Spring 2013).
25. Claudia and Dirk Haarmann, "Basic Income Grant Coalition–Pilot Project" (2012), accessible at http://www.bignam.org/BIG_pilot.html.
26. Margaret Gray, *Labor and the Locavore: Toward a Comprehensive Food Ethic* (Berkeley: University of California Press, 2013).

CHAPTER SIX

1. Tim Jackson, *Prosperity Without Growth: Economics for a Finite Planet* (London: Routledge, 2009).
2. Isabelle Cassiers et al, *Redéfinir la prospérité: Jalons pour un débat public* (La Tour d'Aigues: Edition de l'Aube, 2011).
3. Tyler Cowan, *The Great Stagnation: How America Ate All the Low-Hanging Fruit of Modern History, Got Sick, and Will (Eventually) Feel Better* (New York:

Dutton, 2012). In *The Endless Crisis: How Monopoly-finance Capital Produces Stagnation and Upheaval from the USA to China* (New York: Monthly Review Press, 2012), John Bellamy Foster and Robert McChesney argue that stagnation is the normal state of a mature capitalist economy, dominated by monopolistic firms. Growth can only be squeezed out by desperate or unusual measures, such as government stimuli, increased consumption, bursts of technological innovation, and financial expansion.

4. John Stuart Mill, "Of the Stationary State," in *Principles of Political Economy with Some of Their Applications to Social Philosophy* (1848).
5. Clive Hamilton, *Growth Fetish* (Crows Nest: Allen & Unwin, 2003). Also, see Richard Douthwaite's *The Growth Illusion: How Economic Growth Has Enriched the Few, Impoverished the Many, and Endangered the Planet* (Dublin: Lilliput Press, 1992).
6. Robert Collins, *More: The Politics of Economic Growth in Postwar America* (New York: Oxford University Press, 2000).
7. Quoted in Bill McKibben, *Eaarth: Making a Life on a Tough New Planet* (New York: Holt, 2010), p. 95.
8. Anne Krueger, "Address on Globalization," Seventh St. Petersburg International Economic Forum, International Monetary Fund (June 18, 2003), accessible at http://www.imf.org/external/np/speeches/2003/061803.htm.
9. Donella Meadows, Jørgen Randers, and Dennis Meadows, *Limits to Growth: The 30-Year Update* (New York: Chelsea Green, 2004).
10. The Global Transition to a New Economy (at http://gtne.org) is a project of the New Economics Institute, the New Economics Foundation, Stakeholder Forum for a Sustainable Future, and the Green Economy Coalition. Also, see the principles of the New Economy Working Group at http://www.neweconomyworkinggroup.org/. A project to map various New Economy initiatives in American cities has been launched by the U.S. Solidarity Economy Network, accessible at http://www.shareable.net/blog/how-to-map-the-new-economy-in-your-city. Also see RIPESS at http://www.ripess.org.
11. Some tighter forms of regulation are laid out in Chapter 8 of *Occupy Finance* by the Alternative Banking Group of Occupy Wall Street (September 2013), accessible at http://www. scribd.com/doc/168661471/Occupy-Finance.
12. More systematic treatments of alternative economies include Michael Albert, *Parecon: Life After Capitalism* (New York: Verso, 2003); Gar Alperovitz, *America Beyond Capitalism: Reclaiming Our Wealth, Our Liberty, and Our Democracy* (Boston: Democracy Collaborative Press and Dollars and Sense, 2nd edition, 2011); Richard Wolff, *Democracy at Work: A Cure for Capitalism* (New York: Haymarket, 2012).

13. Mandi Woodruff, "The Numbers Are In: Find Out Just How Many Americans Have Ditched Their Banks," *Business Insider* (January 30, 2012), accessible at http://www.businessinsider.com/the-numbers-are-in-find-out-just-how-many-americans-have-switched-their-banks-2012-1#ixzz2bksiRAQ1.
14. Andrew Grice, "Coalition Will Support Archbishop of Canterbury Justin Welby's Plan for Credit Unions," *The Independent* (July 28, 2013).
15. Ellen Brown, "What We Could Do with a Postal Savings Bank: Infrastructure that Doesn't Cost Taxpayers a Dime," *Global Research* (September 23, 2013), accessible at http://www.globalresearch.ca/what-we-could-do-with-a-postal-savings-bank-infrastructure-that-doesnt-cost-taxpayers-a-dime/5351175.
16. Gar Alperovitz uses his own role as advisor to the steelworkers to launch his survey of the cooperative economy in *What Then Must We Do? Straight Talk about the Next American Revolution* (Washington DC: Chelsea Green, 2013), pp. 28-30.
17. Lavaca Collective, *Sin Patrón: Stories from Argentina's Worker-Run Factories* (New York: Haymarket Books, 2007). See *The Take*, a 2004 documentary by Naomi Klein and Avi Lewis; and Marina Sitrin, *Horizontalism: Voices of Popular Power in Argentina* (Oakland, CA: AK Press, 2007).
18. See the promotional activities of the Public Banking Institute, accessible at http://publicbankinginstitute.org.
19. Writers for the 99 percent, *Occupying Wall Street: The Inside Story of an Action that Changed America* (New York: OR Books, 2011).
20. Astra Taylor, Keith Gessen et al, eds., *Occupy!: Scenes from Occupied America* (New York: Verso Press, 2012).
21. Nathan Schneider, *Thank You, Anarchy: Notes from the Occupy Apocalypse* (Berkeley: University of California Press, 2013); Mark Bray, *Translating Anarchy: The Anarchism of Occupy Wall Street* (London: Zero Books, 2013).
22. The flavor of Occupy was best documented in the movement's own press, which includes *The Occupied Wall Street Journal, Occupy! Gazette, Tidal,* and *The Occupied Times of London.*
23. David Graeber, *The Democracy Project.*

INDEX

ANDREW ROSS is Professor of Social and Cultural Analysis at New York University, and a social activist. A contributor to *The Nation*, the *Village Voice*, *New York Times*, and *Artforum*, he is the author of many books, including, most recently, *Bird on Fire: Lessons from the World's Least Sustainable City* and *Nice Work if You Can Get It*.